THE AWFUL GRAMMAR BOOK

Other titles in this series include

THE AWFUL SPELLERS DICTIONARY
THE AWFUL DRESSMAKER'S BOOK
THE AWFUL COOK'S BOOK
THE AWFUL GARDENER'S BOOK
THE AWFUL MATHEMATICIAN'S BOOK
THE AWFUL MOTORIST'S BOOK
THE AWFUL SECRETARY'S BOOK
THE AWFUL SLIMMER'S BOOK
THE AWFUL PUNTER'S BOOK
THE AWFUL GOLFER'S BOOK
THE AWFUL BOSS'S BOOK
THE AWFUL YACHTSMAN'S BOOK
THE AWFUL ANGLER'S BOOK

72340036 9

3rd Impression 1974

Printed by Stevens Press Limited, Long Eaton
(a member of the Oxley Printing Group Ltd.)

THE AWFUL GRAMMAR BOOK

Sidney Ledson

WOLFE PUBLISHING LTD
10 EARLHAM STREET, LONDON WC2

Introduction

If you have a razor-sharp mind and a photographic memory, you will be an English-language expert in three hours' time; that is how long it takes to read this book and do the exercises. But if you are one of the army of **Awful Grammarians** (and aren't most of us?) you will need a little longer. Indeed, you will probably have to read each section *two* or *three* times.

Unfortunately, the rules for grammar were not drawn up in heaven. The rules have no greater authority than what has been spoken—rightly or wrongly—in the past. However, these past utterings have been sufficiently logical and consistent to form well-defined paths of communication.

The grammarian's job is not simply to *stop* linguistic novelty, but rather to show where the breaking of new ground leads toward a bog; to show which novel twist of usage will weaken the common grid of understanding.

Then again, a grammar book can tell you what is *technically* right or wrong, but it cannot tell you what is *socially* right or wrong. Grammar, like karate, requires discretion in its use. 'Wrong' usage changes to 'right' usage at some unmarked point between Buckingham Palace and the local pub. The expression, 'It is I,' is appropriate to one, 'It's me,' is more suited to the other. While it is admirable to use informal expressions in the interests of friendliness, it is not admirable when they are spoken in ignorance.

When this book has been studied, the reader will be equipped to understand grammar as expressed by its masters: Fowler, Partridge, Vallins and Jespersen; or, if more practical material is desired, the reader is urged to become acquainted with that excellent work *Plain Words* by Sir Ernest Gowers.

SIDNEY LEDSON

Contents

Part One

THE SENTENCE

DEFINITION: **A sentence is a group of words that expresses a complete thought.**

Sentences, like ladies, come in all sizes, shapes and moods. Some express a purpose, 'Put two bob on Late Knight'; some express a hope, 'Dr. Buzzard's fights tooth decay even while you're sleeping'; some are inquisitive, some dictatorial, others poetical. The most common sort of sentence is the kind that makes a statement—as *this* sentence is doing.

The rules for constructing a sentence are simple: begin with a capital letter, express one complete thought, and end with either a full-stop, a question mark or an exclamation mark. Yet people commonly misunderstand what is meant by a complete thought.

Some advertising writers exploit this misunderstanding in the belief that *part*-sentences seem friendlier and make reading easier. The following examples were taken from a single advertisement:—

'Of being the most reliable airline in the world'.

'Also due in no small part to our reputation'.

'Or rather, because it has a small population'.

These are *not* sentences; they are only *parts* of sentences. What is missing? They have no subjects, no topics. Standing alone, each makes an unusual comment *about* something, without telling us *what* this something is. A few words added to these parts of sentences can produce meaningful complete sentences:—

'The title given us, namely that *of being the most reliable airline in the world,* has been revoked following numerous complaints.'

'It is surprising how the mere sight of a thundercloud can produce a run of passenger cancellations, though these are perhaps *also due in no small part to our reputation.*'

'Tristan da Cunha has a small birth-rate because the people are small; *or rather, because it has a small population.*'

Sentences comprise two parts: the subject being discussed, and a story *about* the subject. Consider a simple sentence:—

'Henry swallowed a fly.'

Henry is the topic being discussed; *Henry* is called the **subject.** The rest of the sentence tells a simple story about him. The story part of a sentence is traditionally called the **predicate.** The following sentences have been divided into subjects and predicates in that order. Notice how the subjects increase in length:

Gunpowder/consists of potassium nitrate, charcoal and sulphur.
The island of Krakatau/exploded in 1883.
The sound of this mighty explosion near Sumatra/was heard four hours later, 3,000 miles away.
A smaller explosion which we all experience, namely that of sneezing/expels air at a speed of 100 m.p.h.

You will see that the subject of a sentence can be any length. The longer subjects might appear to be telling a story but, technically, they are merely giving a fuller **description** of the subject. Consider two sentences:—

The Egyptians/invented beer.
Beer/was invented by the Egyptians.

In the first sentence, *Egyptians* is the subject; but in the second, it is part of the story, the predicate. This will serve to remind you that the *role* of a word in a sentence is often determined by its position *in* the sentence rather than by any special quality of the word itself.

There are four kinds of sentences:

STATEMENT: Elephants subsist on roots, twigs, leaves and young shoots.
QUESTION: Why hadn't Tarzan a beard?
COMMAND: Get off the flag, you imbecile!
EXCLAMATION: Triplets, you say!

Subjects or topics are not *always* found at the beginning of sentences. This is particularly true when a question is asked. Such sentences should be rearranged to form **statements** before deciding what the subjects and predicates are:—

What are you doing? = You/are doing what.
Is there a doctor in the house? = A doctor/is there in the house.
When no subject is mentioned in a question-type sentence, the *question-word* becomes the subject.
Who/will know?
What/is going on?
Which/is the best?

In **command** sentences (traditionally called **imperative** sentences), the subject is normally understood to be 'you': Sit down = (You) sit down; Open your mouth = (You) open your mouth; Say 'Ah!' = (You) say 'Ah!'

When the subject consists of several words, there is usually a *single* word among them that tells what is being discussed. These words are italicised in the following sentences:—

A well-educated *person*/employs about 5,000 words in speech.
A quick, brown *frog*/jumps over the crazy dog.

Perhaps you'd like to try your hand at judging groups of words. Here are a few to practise on. Tick off those you think are sentences. But be careful: don't be fooled by the number of words used in any one example; the real test is whether or not a *complete* thought is expressed. **(Answers: page 59).**

1. But Martha is a *fine* name! 2. In the nick of time. 3. Wafted by the breeze 2,000 miles to our foggy shores. 4. Make love, not war. 5. Please do not feed the ducks. 6. Having recorded the amputation of a leg in thirty seconds by a surgeon in Scotland. 7. In the case of Otto Kretschmer, U-boat captain, who sank no less than a quarter of a million tons—45 vessels. 8. To have fiddled while Rome burned. 9. Go! 10. The Honourable Arbeit Q. Smith awaits.

PARTS OF SPEECH

CONSIDERING the thousands of words we use, and the thousands of uses we make of them, it is a wonder that there are only eight distinct jobs for all these words to perform. The eight jobs are called the Parts of Speech; they represent the nuts and bolts, as it were, of every sentence we write or speak. The parts of speech are: **noun, verb, pronoun, adjective, adverb, preposition, conjunction** and **interjection.**

NOUNS

DEFINITION: A **noun** is the name of a person, place, thing, emotion or state.

A *noun* is simply a name. Anything that has a name is a noun. (The words *noun* and *name* come from the same Latin source—*nomen*). Though *you* personally are not a noun, your name *is.* Similarly, everything Man has troubled to name is, by that very action, a noun. You are surrounded by nouns: e.g. *wall, ceiling, floor, window, table, book.* Fully half of the words in your dictionary are simply the names given to things. They are indicated there by the letter *n.*

There are several types of nouns, grouped roughly as follows:—

UNCOMMON NOUNS

Uncommon nouns (traditionally called *proper* nouns) are the names we give to special things—those things that require a capital letter: *Africa, Thursday, Putney, Lord Bertrand Russell, Atlantic Ocean, Coca-Cola.*

COMMON NOUNS

. . . ink, man, rope, cement, rice pudding, sawdust, petrol, kidney, chewing gum. These names do not refer to any special item, but rather to *one* thing in a *class* of items. For example: the name 'man' is shared in common by every adult male human in the world; so it is a common noun.

COLLECTIVE NOUNS

Collective nouns are the names we give to *collections* of things:

e.g. a *forest* is a collection of trees; a *fleet* is a collection of ships. Both *forest* and *fleet* are collective nouns. Others are: *herd* (a collection of animals), *mob, crowd, people, battalion, squad, crew, staff, society, team, group, suite, flock.*

ABSTRACT NOUNS

Just as abstract *art* is difficult to describe, so are abstract nouns. They cannot be seen, heard, smelled, tasted or touched. Most abstract nouns can be grouped loosely under these headings:

QUALITIES: *beauty, patience, integrity, hardness, honesty, durability.*

EMOTIONS: *anger, fear, love, contempt, pity, gratefulness, anxiety.*

STATES: *bachelorhood, friendship, childhood, hunger, death.*

PROCESSES: *dry cleaning, book-binding, day-dreaming, bird-watching.*

When there is only *one* of a noun, it is said to be **singular**—*boy, friendship, fleet*. When there is *more* than one noun, it is said to be **plural**—*boys, friendships, fleets*. The terms **singular** and **plural** are said to indicate the 'number' of a noun.

As you know, the plurals of nouns are formed in several ways. Indeed, there are so many rules governing this, and there are so many exceptions, that it is wiser to consult a dictionary when you are in doubt. Here is the entry for a noun in the *Concise Oxford Dictionary*: wharf (wôrf), n. (pl. *-fs, -ves*). As you see, the word is followed by a pronunciation code, then the small *n* tells us it is a noun: (pl. *-fs, -ves*) tells us the plural form may end with either the letters *fs* or *ves*—*wharfs* or *wharves.*

Sometimes it is difficult to tell whether a word is a noun or not. A simple test is to see if the word can be *made* plural; if it can, it is a noun. For words that are rarely thought of in plural form, a better test is to see whether or not they can provide a topic for conversation; if they can, they are nouns. Fit any such word into the expression 'I'd like to talk about . . .' e.g. *I'd like to talk about carelessness, courage, ugliness, ease, justice, fire-fighting.* All fit; all are nouns.

Of the following ten words, five cannot be nouns. Which are they? **(Answers: page 59.)**

1. dread, 2. nickname, 3. monetary, 4. hard, 5. terrible, 6. summertime, 7. puzzle, 8. instantaneous, 9. corrupt, 10. microphone.

VERBS

DEFINITION: **A verb is a word that expresses action or a state of being.**

Just as there is one word among all others in the subject that names the *topic*, so there is a single word in the predicate that describes the **action** of the subject. Consider the sentence, 'Sound travels at 750 miles per hour.' *Sound* is the subject. What does 'sound' *do* in this sentence? It *travels*. 'Travels' then describes the *action* of the subject. Words that tell what the subjects *do* are called **verbs.**

Some verbs express violent action: *shriek, wrestle, scream*; others are tranquil: *pray, sleep, dream.* Consider the diminishing amount of observable action expressed by these verbs: *fight, leap, shout, run, trot, walk, shuffle, sit, rest, stare, think, wait, hope.* The action of the last few examples is more mental than physical, but this does not lessen their role as verbs.

It might have occurred to you that some verbs could also function as nouns. That is correct. Consider the word *dream* in these sentences.

I dream of Jeannie with the light brown hair.

Coleridge wrote *Kubla Khan* following an opium dream.

'Dream' is the verb of the first sentence. In the second sentence, 'wrote' is the verb, 'dream' is a noun. Many words are similarly able to work as more than one part of speech.

THE OBJECT

DEFINITION: **The object is that thing which receives the action of the verb.**

The **object** is *not* a part of speech. Like the subject, it is a 'position' *filled* by a part of speech in a sentence. You have learned that the verb expresses the *action* of the subject. This action is directed *toward* one thing or object.

Consider the sentence, 'John hit the target.' *John* is the subject. What did John *do*? John *hit*. 'Hit' then is the verb. Now, *what* did John hit? John hit the *target*. 'Target' then is the object that receives the action of the verb; it is called **object** to the verb.

Most sentences contain similar 'targets' or objects of the verb. The object of the verb is always found by asking *What* or *Whom* after the verb: e.g. I dream of *whom*?—*Jeannie*; Coleridge wrote *what*?—*Kubla Khan. Subjects of the verb* and *objects of the verb* are always nouns or the *equivalent* of nouns.

VERB HELPERS

DEFINITION: **Verb helpers are verbs which are joined to other verbs to give different shades of meaning—usually of time.**

The following verbs are often added to other verbs to alter their meanings: *may, might, can, could, will, would, shall, should, do, did, must* and all forms of the verbs *be* and *have*. For example: I *am going* there. She *was talking* to me. I *might have tried* harder. I *had been swimming* in the sea. We *shall have been married* one week in ten minutes' time.

TRAVELLING VERBS

DEFINITION: **Travelling verbs (or transitive verbs) are those which act upon an object.**

Consider the sentence, 'I repaired the car.' 'I' is the subject, 'repaired' is the verb, and 'car' is the target or object. If the object is removed from the sentence—*I repaired*—the result doesn't make sense. Now try this with another sentence, 'I danced the tango.' If we remove the object, *tango*, the result still makes sense—'I danced.'

Verbs that require an object are travelling verbs, or, as they are traditionally called, **transitive** verbs. The action of the subject 'travels over' to an object. Non-travelling verbs—**intransitive** verbs—do not require an object. Most verbs can be used both transitively and intransitively. The verbs in the first three examples below illustrate this. The next three verbs illustrate some of the few cases where a verb can be used only transitively. The final three examples show verbs that can only be used intransitively:—

VERB	TRANSITIVE	INTRANSITIVE
paint	I *paint* pictures.	I *paint*.
swim	I *swim* the breast-stroke.	I *swim*.
run	I *run* five miles a day.	I *run*.
collect	I *collect* stamps.	
throw	I *threw* the boxes away.	
make	I *make* furniture.	
surface		The submarine *surfaced* mid-Atlantic.
smile		She *smiled* instantly.
laugh		We *laughed* heartily.

The last three verbs might appear to have objects, but remember, an object must answer the questions 'what?' or 'whom?'. Any words that follow the verbs *surface*, *smile*, and *laugh* will answer the questions Where, When, Why or How. But in unusual situations, even *these* three verbs might be used transitively: 'We surfaced the wall with gypsum,' 'We laughed a loud laugh,' 'She smiled a sweet smile.' Indeed, there are so *few* verbs that cannot be used both transitively *and* intransitively, that it is wiser to speak of a verb as being *used* transitively or *used* intransitively, rather than saying a verb *is* transitive or *is* intransitive.

How can you put this information to use? Suppose you had heard, and perhaps even used, the word *procrastinate* (to delay, to put off) in the sense 'I had the chance but I procrastinated'. As you see, there is no object—procrastinated *what*?—nothing. You might wonder if the verb can also be used transitively: e.g. 'The judge procrastinated his decision until next Thursday.' 'Decision' is the object of 'procrastinated'—but *is* it correct to use it in this way? By consulting your dictionary you would find an entry similar to that in the *Concise Oxford Dictionary*, reproduced here in part:—

procrăs′ tin|āte, v.i. & t. Defer action, be dilatory . . .

The letters v.i. & t. mean 'verb intransitive and transitive.' We know then that 'procrastinate' *can* be used with or without an object, so our test sentence is correct.

A quick way to determine whether or not a verb *can* be used intransitively is to place it in an intransitive position and see if it stands. Place any verb in the following sentence: 'I . . . for a living. Thus: *I sing, dance, whistle, study, work, play for a living.* They all fit. Try a few others.

LINKING VERBS

For our purpose here, the term 'linking verb' will mean a verb that links the subject to more information *about* the subject. A linking verb will have two qualities: (1) it will express no action that can be exerted upon an object, (2) it will not make sense unless more words follow it.

Mount Everest *is* 29,028 feet high.

Christmas morning *was* a happy occasion.

This soup *tastes* soapy.

Southend *seems* a long way away.

The verbs *is, tastes, was* and *seems* are inactive; they are merely linking the subject in each sentence to further information *about* the subject. Notice in the second sentence that the soup itself does no tasting. The linking verbs you will meet most often are the forms of the verb 'to be'—*am, is, are, was, been, be, were*—plus a few other verbs such as: *becomes, appears, looks, tastes.* However, these last are linking verbs only when the subject of the sentence is *not* active: e.g. 'The weather looks bad.' The 'weather' is not *looking* at anyone or anything. 'Looks' is an idiomatic equivalent of 'is'. Other transitive verbs are sometimes used as linking verbs: e.g. 'It smells delicious;' 'It feels wonderful'.

Because the verbs are inactive in this sort of sentence, the subject can express no power on a target or object. In short, there can be no object. Therefore the words that follow this type of verb are given a special name; they are called the **complement.** Unfortunately, this term is too easily confused with compliment. A better term might be **balance,** because the information that follows a linking verb, in a sense, balances the subject.

Mount Everest = 29,028 feet high.

Christmas morning = a happy occasion.

This soup = soapy.

Southend = a long way away.

Sentences containing a linking verb can usually be inverted (reversed) and still give a balanced meaning without the addition of a verb-helper:—

Joshua Slokum was the first man to sail around the world alone.
The first man to sail around the world alone was Joshua Slokum.

In the following sentences, two verbs are used transitively, two are used intransitively and two are linking verbs. Can you recognise each? **(Answers: page 59.)**

1. I am going home. 2. The ministers are in conference. 3. Dogs bark for Bone-Biks. 4. The speed of the Atlantic sailfish is almost 70 mph. 5. Win an expense-free trip to the North Pole. 6. Mild tobacco promotes mild cancer.

PRONOUNS

DEFINITION: **a pronoun is a word used in place of a noun.**

Just as film-stars have stand-ins, so do nouns. A word that 'stands-in' for a noun is called a **pronoun.** How can a word stand-in for another? Consider the sentence 'I hear reindeer on the roof.' We could also say, 'Reindeer—I hear *them* on the roof.' The word *them* stands for reindeer; it has 'stood-in'. Here are three more examples: 'The anaconda is the world's longest snake; *it* is found in S. America.' (*it* = anaconda). 'Henry has strange tastes: *he* likes strawberry jam on his kippers.' (*he* = Henry). 'This amazing new dentifrice not only protects your teeth, *it* protects your tooth-brush too.' (*it* = dentifrice).

Any word that can stand-in for a noun is a pronoun; that will include the following: *I, me, we, us, you, he, him, she, her, it, they, them.*

Two strange cases

You will recall that both the subject and the object in a sentence must be a noun or its equivalent. *Pronouns* are noun-equivalents; therefore they can act as subjects or objects. But a unique rule governs the use of pronouns. Whereas a noun retains the *same* form when working as a subject or object (The *trees* fell down. I fell *trees*.), pronouns *change* their form. We say 'He saw me,' but we cannot say 'Me saw he.' Why not?

The answer involves **cases.** But these are not like violin cases or cigarette cases: they are the **case of the subject** and the **case of the object.** However, the word **'role'** would be clearer, for *that* is the intended meaning—'role' or 'position'. When a word is used as the *subject* of a sentence, it is said to be in the *subjective* role: a word used as the *object* is said to be in the *objective* role. Pronouns are divided into two groups: those that may be used as subjects, and those that may be used as objects. Here is how they are divided:—

SUBJECTIVE	OBJECTIVE
I	me
we	us
you	you
he	him
she	her
it	it
they	them

As you see, the pronouns *you* and *it* behave like nouns—they remain unchanged in the subjective and objective roles. All the rest must abide by the rules and be used only for the job allotted them. You can test the correctness of this division by placing suitable pronouns in the sentence 'Subject saw Object'—*I saw you, We saw them*, etc.—avoiding, of course, pairs that are related: I—me, I—us, and such.

Exceptions

It was mentioned earlier that the linking verbs (am, is, are, was, been, be, were, becomes, appears, looks, tastes) create special difficulties. They do indeed—beginning now.

Unlike other verbs, linking verbs cannot be followed by an object. Instead, they are followed by a balance or complement. To maintain proper balance then, the balance must be *subjective*, not objective; so while a normal verb takes an objective form of a pronoun (It helps *her*), the linking verb requires that the pronoun be in its *subjective* form (It is *she*). That is why the following expressions are technically correct: *I am he, It is I, It was she, It was they, It was we*. (This rule doesn't apply when the linking verb is merely helping a normal verb: e.g. We *are going* to see her; They *are visiting* him; They *were telling* me, etc).

What are we to think about such expressions? G. H. Vallins has this to say: 'But the fact remains that few people would say or write "It's I," "This is he," "That's she." Usage, a trifle shamefacedly, admits the object-form to such expressions, "It's me," "This is him," "That's her," perhaps because it can more easily bear the stress. In any case, these expressions belong almost entirely to the spoken tongue. They are rarely seen in writing, and so pass muster with those who, seeing them, might condemn them.'

One strange attempt at correctness occurs when two pronouns are linked by *and*: 'They gave her and I the afternoon off.' Remove the words 'her and' from the sentence, and it will become obvious that 'me' is the correct form. This '*and-me* fright' probably springs from over-correction of childhood errors—'Her and me are going to the pictures'—where both 'her' and 'me' are objective pronoun forms placed in a subjective role. As a result of this, many people feel uncomfortable about the use of 'and me', 'and her', 'and him'.

All the following sentences are correct. Where usage seems questionable, remove one or other of the pronouns and test the sentence.

He took her and me to London.
The harp belongs to her and him.
I saw him and her yesterday.
Herbert and she want a hippopotamus for Christmas.
She, he and I are going on holiday with them.

What about the sentence, 'She, George and *myself* will be taking tea together'? Pronouns such as *myself, yourself, himself* are called **reflexive**—though **reflective** might be more readily understood. Such pronouns reflect or 'mirror' the action of the verb back to the subject: 'I cut myself.' They have one other correct use: to underline or intensify a noun or pronoun: 'George himself dropped the cake.' However, 'myself' is *not* correct when used as a simple substitute for *me* or, as in the opening sentence, as a substitute for *I*. This same rule will apply to 'you', which should have been used in the following sentence, 'This is for yourself.'

DESCRIBERS

The job of some words is to describe *other* words. These descriptive words form two separate groups; one group describes *things* (nouns and pronouns), the second group describes *verbs.*

ADJECTIVES

DEFINITION: **An adjective describes or limits the meaning of a noun or pronoun. Adjectives tell 'what kind of', 'which one' or 'how many'.**

By placing adjectives in front of a noun, we can change or limit the noun's meaning—a *big* house, a *small* house, a *new* house, an *old* house, a *haunted* house. The word 'adjective' is not an apt name, but we must remember it because dictionaries refer to thing-describers by the abbreviation *adj.*

The most common adjectives are 'a', 'an' and 'the'. They have special titles. 'A' and 'an' refer to no particular thing; accordingly, they are called the **indefinite articles**—a seemingly long-winded title for such short words. Perhaps this mis-match will make the term easy to remember. '*A* house' refers to *any* house: nothing could be more indefinite than that. 'A' is used with words beginning with a consonant *sound*; 'an' is used with words beginning with a vowel sound. It is the sound *alone* which determines the aptness of *a* or *an,* not the spelling; hence '*a* hero'; but '*an* honour'. 'A' and 'an' are forms of the numeral 'one'; for this reason it is as correct to say 'a hundred' as 'one hundred'.

'The' is a very definite term: '*the* house' is that *one* house we have discussed or have seen; it cannot be confused with any other house on earth. Accordingly, 'the' is called the **definite** article.

The words 'this', 'that', 'these', 'those' point to things. They are called **demonstrative** adjectives. If the word 'demonstrative' can help you think of 'pointing', then it is a useful one. Assuredly, *people* who 'demonstrate' do a great deal of pointing. (*Note:* sometimes these four words are not adjectives, but pronouns: e.g. 'Those were the good old days.' Here, the word 'those' is the subject of the sentence—and the subject of a sentence must be a noun or its equivalent. Again, 'That is the way to do it': 'that' is the subject pronoun. But if we said 'Those days . . .' or 'That way . . .' then *those* and *that* would be adjectives again).

Some adjectives show ownership: *my* looks, *your* brains, *our* talent, *his* money, *her* charm, *their* admiration, *its* suitability. These are called, aptly enough, **possessive adjectives.** But these should not be confused with *mine, yours, ours, hers, theirs,* which are not adjectives but pronouns. (The forms *his* and *its* do not change). Remember, an adjective *describes,* but a pronoun *stands-in.* 'Your car is new; *mine* is old'—*mine* is standing-in for 'my car'.

Numbers are sometimes used as adjectives: one horse, two cows, three chickens. These indicate a definite quantity. Other words, *some, a few, either, each, both, all, every, many, most,* are adjectives used to express quantities. Colours are usually adjectives, We don't normally buy *red* or *black*, but rather red or black *things*—red *paint*, black *silk*, purple *shirt*.

Some adjectives are used for comparing one noun to another: 'That spice is hot' (notice the linking verb), 'That spice is hotter,' 'That spice is hottest.' *Hot*, *hotter* and *hottest* are called **positive**, **comparative** and **superlative** adjectives respectively. The comparative form is used to show a relationship between only two things.

> **WRONG:** He is the younger of the three brothers. (Use *youngest*)
>
> The superlative form is used between *more* than two things.
>
> **WRONG:** Of the two fish, this is the largest. (Use *larger*)

Some adjectives show comparative and superlative forms by the addition of *more* and *most*: e.g. *hopeful, more hopeful, most hopeful*. The rule determining *which* form an adjective takes for comparison is indefinite, but in general, words of *one* syllable—*cold, big, small*—add a tail: e.g. *cold, colder, coldest*. Words of *three* syllables employ *more* and *most*. Words of *two* syllables vary.

Some adjectives cannot sanely be compared. A thing can be perfect, or it can be *less* than perfect, but it cannot be *more* than perfect; therefore we can say *almost* or *nearly* perfect, but not *more* perfect or *most* perfect. This same logic applies to the following: *basic, complete, empty, essential, fatal, final, full, fundamental, ideal, impossible, obvious, pure, unique*. As a diversion, you might puzzle out better ways of expressing the ideas that prompt misuse of these words, e.g. 'more fatal' wishes to convey 'more toxic' or 'more poisonous'.

Sometimes even nouns can be used as adjectives—'an apple tree'. Here, *apple* is describing the tree. In 'a summer day', *summer* tells us what *sort* of day it is; therefore it is an adjective. Other examples: *river's bed* (showing possession too!), *mahogany table, banana peel, office party, day's end*.

Adjectives are not always placed *before* the thing they describe. This is particularly true when they are describing pronouns instead of nouns. Not only do they *follow* the pronoun but they are separated from it by a linking verb: 'He is tall,' 'She is sweet,' 'They are happy.' Think of these expressions in the terms of 'tall he', 'sweet she' and 'happy they.'

Adjectives can be strung together: e.g. 'That great, hulking brute is my husband.' Here we have three adjectives telling the particular brute in question: he is *that* brute, a *great* brute, and a *hulking* brute. Notice that 'that' does *not* describe 'great,' nor does 'great' describe 'hulking'; they each act solely upon the noun.

If you turn back to the ten-word test following *Nouns*, you will find that the five words which are not nouns, are adjectives.

ADVERBS

DEFINITION: **An adverb describes or limits verbs, adjectives, and**

other adverbs. Adverbs tell Where, When, Why, How, and 'to what extent'.

Just as adjectives describe nouns and pronouns, so other words describe or limit the action of verbs: e.g. 'He swam *quickly*. 'Quickly' describes the swimming, tells *how* he swam. The root meaning of the word adverb is 'add-to-verb'; however, this is only part of an adverb's job.

Let us look at three sentences mentioned earlier: 'The submarine surfaced mid-Atlantic,' 'She smiled instantly,' and 'We laughed heartily.' It will be obvious now that the words following the verbs are adverbs—'mid-Atlantic' tells *where* the submarine surfaced, 'instantly' tells *when* she smiled, 'heartily' tells *how* we laughed.

Were we to say, 'The submarine surfaced mid-Atlantic to recharge its batteries,' we would add another adverb to the sentence telling *why* the submarine surfaced. Or again, if we said 'The submarine partially surfaced mid-Atlantic to recharge its batteries,' we would add still another adverb to the sentence—an adverb which tells *to what extent* the submarine surfaced.

This then is the way adverbs describe or limit the action of a verb—by answering the questions *where, when, why, how* and *to what extent*. But adverbs are able to limit adjectives and other adverbs as well as verbs.

Consider the sentence, 'The iron is hot.' Here, 'hot', following a linking verb, is an adjective describing *iron*—'hot iron'. Now if we say, 'The iron is *very* hot,' 'very' cannot describe iron as a 'very iron'; it describes 'hot'—tells *how* hot; therefore we have an adverb describing an adjective.

Take the sentence 'He walked slowly.' 'Slowly' is an adverb telling *how* he walked. But if we say 'He walked *very* slowly,' the word 'very' has nothing to do with the verb 'walked'—one cannot 'very walk'—'very' tells us *to what extent* or *how* slowly he walked. It describes or limits 'slowly'; therefore we have an adverb describing another adverb.

In the sentence, 'You were entirely correct,' (linking verb), 'correct' is an adjective describing the subject 'you'. 'Entirely' tells *to what extent* the person was correct; therefore it is an adverb describing an adjective. Other adverbs that tell 'to what extent,' or 'to what degree' are: *almost, nearly, partly, completely, barely, very much, once, four times.*

The combination of adverb, adjective and noun is one we make great use of in our daily conversations. The following examples will serve to remind you of these relationships; they are adverb, adjective and noun in that order: *rather pleasant day; quite wet weather; very high humidity; exceptionally dry month; wonderfully warm day; truly fine summer; terribly short dress.*

Many adverbs can be recognised by their *–ly* endings: *sadly, happily, separately, generally, presumably, rarely, usually, fully, occasionally;* others are not so easily spotted: *always, sometimes, seldom, somewhat.* Other adverbs have –ly endings that are sometimes dropped: *run quick(ly), smell sweet(ly), fight fair(ly), travel light(ly), go slow(ly)*.

'Not' is a particularly important adverb—'I have not seen him,' = 'I have seen him not.' *To what extent* have I seen him?—*not* at all.

Adverbs change form for comparison in almost the same way as adjectives do: *fast, faster; intelligently, more intelligently, most intelligently.*

PREPOSITIONS

DEFINITION: **A preposition joins a noun or pronoun to some other word in a sentence and tells what the relationship is between the two joined words.**

Consider the following two sentences: The natives made soup *for* him. The natives made soup *of* him. The words 'for' and 'of' are used to join the pronoun 'him' to the noun-object of the sentence, 'soup'. These joining words are called prepositions. A preposition can join pronouns *or* nouns to other sentence-words: I nailed the lid *with* my landlord. I nailed the lid *on* my landlord. Here, the prepositions 'with' and 'on' join the noun 'landlord' to the noun-object 'lid'.

This then is the main job of a preposition—to introduce and join a noun or pronoun to some other word in a sentence. But as the four examples show, prepositions do much more than introduce and join. they also show the *relationship* between the words so joined. This is the dual role of prepositions: to join nouns and pronouns to other words, and to explain what the relationship *is* between the joined words.

Some of the most common prepositions are also the shortest words in our language: *to, by, at, in, on, of, up*—and they are easily recognised. But shortness is not a necessary feature of prepositions; indeed, some are composed of several words—*in the middle of, at the back of.* The main common feature of prepositions is that they express a **relationship**; sometimes it is a relationship of position, or perhaps a relationship of time; or again, movement, ownership, or attitude.

There are a great many prepositions—far too many to memorise—and some of them occasionally work as another part of speech; therefore a good number of examples will be given so you can develop a sense of the preposition's work. Go over the following groups slowly, and study the relationships effected by the prepositions:—

> back *from* the farm; going *to* the circus; fell *in* the ocean; chip *off* the block; boy *with* the dog; gift *for* his mother; holiday *during* the winter; rolled *under* the table; disappeared *over* the hill; race *across* the country; flew *above* the clouds; space *between* the buildings; man *beside* the helicopter; house *among* the trees; price *beyond* our means; step *toward* his goal; travel *along* the street; look *like* a horse; mountain *near* the sea; shot

through the heart; climbed *into* the cockpit; conduct *beneath* his dignity; truth *behind* the story; lawn *outside* the castle.

Here are a few of the multiple-word prepositions: in *front of, ahead of, because of, by means of, contrary to, in addition to, in place of, in spite of, as far as, according to.*

PHRASES

DEFINITION: **A phrase consists of a preposition and a noun or pronoun, e.g. 'in the morning'; which, considered as a whole, can act as a noun, adverb or adjective.**

'Phrase' is the name given to the preposition *and* the noun or pronoun it introduces: *at the fair, by him, on the wagon.* A phrase may also contain words that describe its noun or pronoun: *under a wonderfully luminous moon; with long, white dangling tassels; at an old, creaking, long-forgotten mill.*

A preposition is said to *govern* the noun or pronoun in its phrase; in fact, the noun or pronoun in the phrase is said to be the *object* of the preposition. It stands to reason then that a pronoun-object of a preposition will need be in its *objective* form; so whereas we say 'It is I,' we say 'It is *for me.*' *Me* is the object of 'for'. Again, 'I believe they are with her and him.' The preposition 'with' requires the *objective* form of pronoun be used rather than the *subjective* form. Objects of a preposition answer the questions What or Whom in the same way sentence objects answer these questions for the verb.

The type of phrase we have covered, the prepositional phrase, is used to *describe.* They are really no more than enlarged adverbs and adjectives. Consider the sentence, 'The person with the long, blond hair is my father.' Here, 'with the long, blond hair' describes the noun 'person'; it is acting like an adjective; therefore we say it is an *adjective phrase.* Phrases are not always so easy to categorise, but there is a rule that can help us.

The rule says that a phrase is the *equivalent* of any word that can *replace* it; therefore, if the meaning of a phrase can be expressed by an adjective, it must be an adjective phrase; or if it can be replaced by an adverb, it is an adverb phrase. Let us put this to the test:—

'She smiled in a charming manner'—'in a charming manner' is a phrase. The meaning of the phrase can be conveyed almost as well by the word 'charmingly'. 'Charmingly' answers the question 'how' for the verb 'smiled'; therefore it is an adverb. And so, 'in a charming manner' must be an adverb phrase. Try another:—

'I will see you in the morning.' 'In the morning' is a phrase. With small licence, it could be replaced by the word 'tomorrow'. 'Tomorrow' answers the question When for the verb 'see'; therefore it is an adverb. So the phrase 'in the morning' must be an adverb phrase.

Sometimes, when there is a variety of descriptive material in a phrase, it is difficult to settle on a single word that expresses the full meaning of the phrase. 'With the long, blond hair' is such a phrase.

Here we need choose just *one* of the words as the basis for a describer—'The *hairy* man is my father.' Try yet another:—

'The girl in the slinky, black evening dress is Suzy.' 'In the slinky, black, evening dress' is the phrase. By substituting the single word 'slinky', or 'beautiful', or 'attractive' we determine that it is an adjective phrase. True, the black evening dress has not been mentioned, but the spirit of the phrase is expressed, and that is all we require.

A general sort of word is also needed to test phrases expressing *location*: e.g. 'He threw three coins and his wife into the fountain.' 'Into the fountain' is a phrase; but what single word can replace it? Well, suppose you were standing beside the fountain; you could point to the spot and say, 'He threw three coins and his wife *here* (or *there*).' The word 'here' or 'there' will serve as a one-word equivalent for any phrase expressing location. 'There' answers the question Where for any verb, and so indicates an adverb phrase.

'There' will replace phrases such as: *in the jungle; up the creek; over the rainbow; down the spout; into the breach; beyond the fringe.*

Similarly, the word 'then' can become a one-word replacement for any phrase expressing time: *after the rain; until the winter; in the evening; before Easter; between Christmas and New Year; on my birthday; for the moment; on time.* And because 'then' answers When to any verb, the phrase it replaces must be an adverb phrase.

Phrases describing *manner* may require some invention to determine a one-word substitute.

He shut the door *with a great slam.*—'loudly', answers How.

She sings *in an irritatingly forced manner.*—'terribly', answers How.

He ended the game *in a rage.*—'angrily', answers How.

Any word or phrase that answers How is, of course, adverbial; the same applies to any word or phrase that expressed a reason; but here, it isn't possible to find a one-word substitute.

It's said they married *for income tax reasons.*

He has begun weight-lifting *for his health.*

If the phrase answers Why, it is adverbial.

When phrases follow one another, it is sometimes difficult to classify one or other of them. Consider the sentence, 'We buy our spirits at the shop at the corner.' There are two phrases here: 'at the shop' and 'at the corner'. The first phrase is easy to identify; it answers the question Where; therefore it is an adverb phrase. However, it might be said that 'at the corner' *also* answers the question Where and is, therefore, also adverbial. That is true; but we need ask is this the *intended* meaning of the phrase, or is it meant to tell us *where* the shop is—telling us, in effect, *which* shop? This seems more likely; the sentence would convey the same message thus: 'We buy our spirits at the corner shop'; therefore 'at the corner' is an adjective phrase.

What about the sentence, 'Our friends live at the corner over the shop'? An 'over the shop' corner seems absurd at first; but what is the *intended* meaning? They live at the *shop*-corner, not the *bank*-corner nor the *petrol-station* corner, nor the *vacant-lot* corner; therefore 'over the shop' tells us *which one*—it is an adjective phrase.

In the previous two sentences, both phrases seemed to answer the question Where; however, it was decided that the *intended* meaning of one was to narrow or limit the meaning of the other. Consider this sentence: 'She spoke with great speed in a low voice.' Both answer the question How. Does one phrase narrow or limit the meaning of the other? Let us reduce the phrases to single words and see: 'She spoke quickly, quietly.' It will be seen that each phrase has its own effect upon the verb 'spoke'—both are adverbial.

Let us consider some adjective phrases.

The Sunday morning cricket game is fun.
The game *of cricket, on Sunday morning*, is fun.

The two phrases in the second sentence, 'of cricket' and 'on Sunday morning', are doing the same work as the noun-adjectives (nouns used as adjectives) 'Sunday morning' and 'cricket' in the first sentence; therefore they are both adjective phrases. Try to determine the kinds of phrases found in the following sentences. Where two phrases run together, they are separated by an oblique stroke.

The girls *from St. Trinian's* are arriving *in a tank.*
Light travels *at a speed/of 186,000 miles per second.*
The rain *in Spain* stays mainly *in the plain.*

Here are the answers along with the thinking that determined them: 'from St. Trinian's'—*what* kind of girls?—*St. Trinian* girls—adjective phrase; 'in a tank'—arriving *how*?—in a tank—adverb phrase; 'at a speed/of 186,000 miles per second'—the second phrase can be replaced by the word 'phenomenal', 'at a phenomenal speed'; therefore it is an adjective phrase describing the noun 'speed'. By helping to complete the meaning of the first phrase in this way, 'at a phenomenal speed' can be replaced by 'quickly'—an adverb answering How. 'At a speed' is therefore an adverb phrase. 'In Spain'—*what* sort of rain?—*Spanish* rain—adjective phrase; 'in the plain'—the rain stays mainly *where*?—*in the plain*—adverb phrase.

Whenever you have difficulty determining what job a phrase performs, stop and decide what its *intended* meaning is: e.g. what kind of phrase have we in this sentence, 'Your holiday resort has been carefully selected *by travel agents*'? The phrase 'by travel agents' means to tell you the resort has been selected by experts. 'By experts' is itself a phrase which can be replaced by 'expertly': 'Your holiday resort has been selected carefully and expertly.' 'Expertly' answers 'how' to the verb 'has been selected'. It is adverbial, and so is the phrase 'by travel agents'.

Diagrams

Words and phrases are much easier to classify if we analyse

them by use of diagrams. Besides, it's fun.

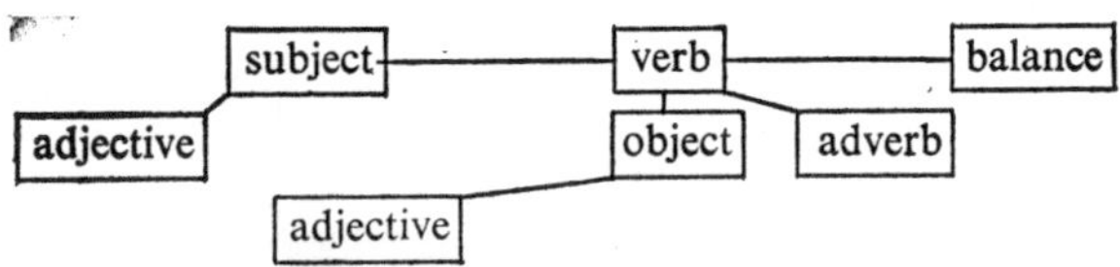

This is the basic grid. Obviously, if a verb takes an object, it will *not* take a complement and vice versa; however, having separate positions for each will serve to remind you to watch for the differences. All adjectives are connected by an oblique stroke running to the left; adverbs are connected by an oblique stroke to the right. Let us analyse a simple sentence: 'A pint of milk contains 378 calories.'

What is the subject—'pint' or 'milk'? The preposition 'of' makes 'milk' *objective*; therefore it cannot be the subject of the sentence. 'Pint' is the subject, 'of milk' is an adjective phrase telling us what sort of pint it is. 'A' is another adjective telling us that only *one* pint is being considered.

'Contains' is the verb. It is a linking verb? Could we consider the sentence thus: A pint of milk = 378 calories? We might be tempted. Whenever you are in doubt, consult your dictionary. 'Contain' is a transitive verb; therefore it requires an object.

A pint of milk contains *what*?—calories, the object; *how many* calories?—378, a number adjective. Here is the way the information would be shown.

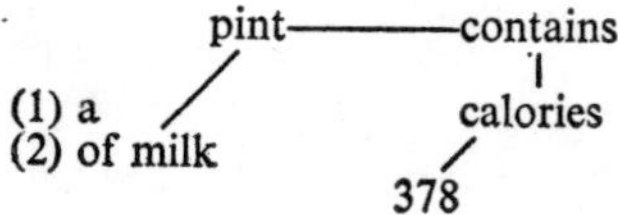

Try another: 'There are over 700,000 recordings in the BBC phono library.' The only word preceding the verb is 'there', but this is obviously not the topic of the sentence. 'Recordings' is the subject; 'there' merely tells *where* the recordings are. When a sentence begins with 'there', re-arrange the sentence before analysing it: thus, 'Over 700,000 recordings are there in the BBC phono library.'

'Recordings' is the subject; '700,000' is a number adjective telling *how many* recordings; 'over' is an adverb which adds greater meaning to '700,000'. 'Are' is the verb—a *linking* verb—therefore the sentence has a balance or complement. 'There' is an adverb giving direction to the verb 'are'. 'In the BBC phono collection' is a phrase in balance. When the balance forms a single unit in this way, it is not necessary to analyse its parts. Here is how the sentence would be shown:

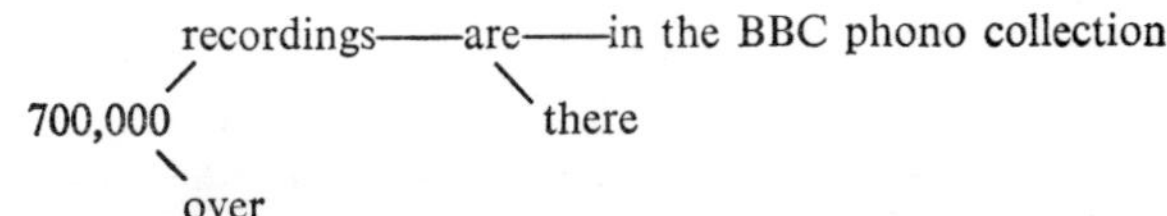

Let us analyse a question-type sentence: 'How do they get new tube trains down the escalators?' This sentence needs re-arranging before analysis: 'They do get new tube trains down the escalators how.'

'They' is the subject; 'do get' is the combination verb; 'tube trains' is the object. 'New' is an adjective describing the tube trains. 'Down the escalators' is a phrase limiting the verb 'do get'. It is therefore adverbial. 'How' is another adverb limiting the meaning of the verb. Here is the diagram:

they———do get
tube trains (1) down the escalators
(2) how
new

NOTE: Most expressions of exclamation cannot be analysed: e.g. 'Blast!' 'The ruddy cheek!' Such expression are only *parts* of a sentence.

Here are eleven sentences for you to analyse by diagram. As you finish each analysis, compare your diagrams with that on page 59.

1. The organ in Liverpool Cathedral has 10,936 pipes. 2. The sun never sets on my Gin (from a spirit advertisement). 3. In pre-Christian times, the traditional December celebration marked the winter solstice. 4. The last pitched battle in England was on Drummossie Moor, Inverness-shire, in 1746. 5. Dogs are not allowed in the shop. 6. The world's largest salt mine, in Ohio, U.S.A., produces 12,000 tons per day. 7. The London Transport two-hour circular tour of the landmarks of London covers twenty miles. 8. Enjoy real Continental cooking with local dishes. 9. Swedes consume, on the average, 26 pounds of coffee per person per year. 10. Simply fill in the application form below. 11. Watch the graceful progress of the timeless gondolas along the legend-haunted canals of beautiful Venice.

SUGGESTION

IF YOU CONFUSE some of the terms that have been covered up to this point, or mistake some of their applications, then you are quite normal. Grammar *is* puzzling and complicated. You will find Part Two much simpler if you undertake a review of all earlier material before continuing.

Part Two

PERSON

MOST OF THE PRONOUNS covered so far have been stand-ins for *persons*—I, you, he, she, and etc. Because they represent persons, they are called **personal pronouns.** Regarded thus, almost as people, they are given names so we can tell *what* person is being referred to. For example, the pronoun 'I' is considered to be the 'first' person, and because it can refer to only *one* person rather than several, 'I' is called the first person **singular** form of the personal pronouns.

The pronoun 'we' refers to both 'you' and 'I'. 'We' is called the **first person** form too. But because *two* persons are referred to, 'we' is called the first person **plural** form.

The word 'you' is called the **second** person. Is 'you' singular or plural? Well, it will depend on whether you are speaking to *one* person or several, won't it? At one time, the English language had the word 'thou' for use when speaking to one person, and 'ye' for speaking to *more* than one person; but now the word 'you' must do both jobs. Technically, 'you' is a *plural* form; however, it sees greater use in the one-person role, so 'you' will be called *singular* here. (Confusion cannot arise from this novelty because there is no other second-person pronoun to confuse it with).

'He' refers to a third person, usually absent; therefore 'he' is the **third person** form. And because 'he' is just *one* person, 'he' is third person **singular.** Similarly, 'she' is also third person singular.

The words 'one', 'someone', 'somebody', 'everyone', 'no one' are all singular, and again, third-person in form. The word 'it', though not normally used for referring to people, is also third person singular.

When we speak of *more* than one absent person—'they'—the term is third person **plural.** Here are the personal pronouns with their proper names.

I—first person, singular
we—first person, plural
they—third person, plural
you—second person, singular
he/she/one/it—third person, singular

However, these are the *subjective* forms of the personal pronouns, aren't they? These are the forms we would use for the *subject* of a sentence, or in the balance (complement) of a linking verb. For this reason, the words *subjective role* (or *case*) should follow each of the above terms.

Now consider the *objective* roles of the personal pronouns. 'Me' is called ***first person, singular, objective role.*** 'You' keeps the same form for both roles. 'Us' is ***first person, plural, objective role.*** What would the terms be for 'him', and 'her', and 'them'?

ANOTHER LOOK AT VERBS

Verbs have always been considered the most important word in sentences. In fact, the word 'verb' comes from the Latin *verbum*, meaning simply 'word'. Verbs are thus *the* sentence words; they are the motors that give movement to sentences; they are the activators, the doing-words. It is perhaps fitting that so important a group of words should have complicated works and workings. Let us consider what these are.

Person

A personal pronoun lends its 'person' to the verb that suits it: e.g. 'I try'—the verb *try* is in the form suited for the first person singular pronoun, so *try* is called the first person singular form of the verb. Here are the names for the other personalised verb forms:—

1st person singular—I try
1st person plural—We try
2nd person singular—You try
3rd person singular—He/she/one/it tries
3rd person plural—They try

All verb forms are the same except that of 3rd person singular—*tries*. This difference is normal with all verbs: e.g. I/you/we/they *see*, but he/she *sees*; I/you/we/they *go*, but he/she *goes*. Third person singular is also the form used for all singular nouns—*A root tries to anchor the plant securely while searching for food.* Plural nouns use the third person plural form—*Birds try to find protected spots for nesting.*

Time

Verbs change their form for different time; they are said to have 'tense'. The word **tense** comes from the Latin *tempus*—which means 'time'. Strictly speaking, the word *tense* as it is used in grammar, means *more* than 'time'; but from a layman's position, the difference doesn't justify use of an obscure term where a familiar one will do.

Verbs have three times: e.g. **I saw; I see; I shall see.** The first expression tells what happened in the past: it is called the **past time** of the verb. The second expression tells what is happening at the present; it is called the **present time** of the verb. The third expression tells what will happen in the future; it is called the **future time** of the verb. *Will* and *shall* are the verb helpers that make the expression of future time possible. (For correct use of *will* and *shall*, see page 56). Now let us consider these three times in detail.

Present time

I see it; I am seeing it; I have seen it. The first sentence 'I see it,' is simple and straightforward; it is, in fact, called the **present simple time.** The second sentence, 'I am seeing it,' emphasises the fact that the 'seeing' is continuing even while it is being reported. This is called the **present continuing time.**

In the third sentence, 'I have seen it,' the 'seeing', though again simple, has been finished or completed; but completed *when*—ten minutes ago? yesterday? last week? That part isn't definite; the *degree* of 'pastness' is uncertain. What *is* certain is the fact that the 'seeing' has been completed at the time the sentence is uttered. For that reason, the verb-form is called **present completed time** (or traditionally, **present perfect tense).**

Past time

Now look at the sentences, *I saw it; I was seeing it; I had seen it.* 'I saw it' is *past simple time.* In the sentence 'I was seeing it,' we get the impression that the speaker is going to tell us something more, and that this unmentioned event occurred at the time the 'seeing' was still going on. In other words, the 'seeing' is a reference point for something still to be mentioned. Let us test this with another sentence: 'It was snowing dreadfully when he called.' His 'call' has been related to 'snowing' which was in progress or continuing at the time of the call. This verb-form is **past continuing time.**

In 'I had seen it,' the speaker is again going to tell us something more, but he wants us to know that the 'seeing' had ended before the other event occurred. 'It had snowed dreadfully the night he called;' the snowing had ended—had been completed—before he called. This verb form is **past completed time** (traditionally, **past perfect tense**).

Future time

I shall see him; I shall be seeing him; I shall have seen him. The first example is **future simple time.** The second sentence employs the form we use to relate a future 'happening' to a future date, or to some other future event: e.g. *I shall be seeing him this afternoon,* or *tomorrow,* or *next week.* 'Seeing' will be continuous throughout our meeting. This verb-form is the **future continuing time.**

In 'I shall have seen him,' the speaker is not telling us when the 'seeing' will happen; instead he is telling us when the seeing will be *completed*: e.g. 'I shall have seen him by Thursday.' This might be interpreted as 'I may see him Monday, Tuesday or Wednesday—I don't know which—but by Thursday, the seeing will be finished.' This is **future completed time.**

There they are, three times—*past, present* and *future*—each with its three types of action: *simple* action, *continuing* action and *completed* action. But there is one more type of action; it is a *mixture* of continuing action and completed action—*I have been seeing him; I had been seeing him; I shall have been seeing him:—*

I have been seeing him: The 'seeing' has occurred and been completed one or more times up to the present moment, and will probably continue similarly in the future; therefore the action is truly completed and continuing. This verb form is the **present completed continuing.**

I had been seeing him: The speaker is going to tell us something more—some information he wants to relate to the time of the 'seeing': e.g. 'I had been seeing him for a week when the police dropped in unexpectedly.' The 'seeing' had occurred one or more times up to the moment the police dropped in. This verb-form is the **past completed continuing.**

I shall have been seeing him: Again, the speaker has more to add. He is going to tell us what a succession of past 'seeings,' present 'seeings' and future 'seeings' will total at some future time when they are added up: e.g. 'I shall have been seeing him perform this same trick fifty times by tonight.' This verb form, **future completed continuing time,** is commonly used to express length of residence, i.e. 'We shall have been living in England ten years next month.'

Here is a list of the verb forms now covered, shown, this time, in 3rd person singular form.

SIMPLE		CONTINUING
He sees	PRESENT	He is seeing
He saw	PAST	He was seeing
He will see	FUTURE	He will be seeing
He has seen	PRESENT COMPLETED	He has been seeing
He had seen	PAST COMPLETED	He had been seeing
He will have seen	FUTURE COMPLETED	He will have been seeing

The following exercise will help you sort out the various verb-forms in your mind. Make certain you locate the true subject of each sentence before attempting to name the verb-form. To find the subject, ask Who or What plus the verb: e.g. 'Frank swam the Channel.' 'Swam' is the verb. *Who* swam? Frank. Another: 'His opinion doesn't count for much here.' 'Doesn't count' is the verb. *What* doesn't count? Opinion.

Give the person, number (singular or plural), time and action of the italicised verbs: (EXAMPLE: If I *kiss* you good night, *will* you please *go* home? verb: kiss (subject 'I')—1st person singular, present, simple. verb: will go (subject 'you')—2nd person singular, future, simple). **(Answers: page 61.)**

1. *Are* you *having* any fun? 2. A stitch in time *saves* nine. 3. They *are* only *trying* their best. 4. *Have* you *taken* your medicine? 5. It is estimated that buildings *will* one day *rise* to 400 storeys. 6. She *had been having* shock treatment to cure athlete's foot. 7. The gut from Spanish silkworms *provides* material for surgical stitching. 8. We *had* only *been* in the gallery ten minutes when

the painting vanished. 9. Where *have* all the young girls *gone?* 10. They *have been trying* to telephone us for an hour. 11. He *will have been speaking* for an hour soon.

Active and Passive Voice

The use of the word 'voice' here is deceptive; the word 'role' again provides a better description. You will recall that transitive verbs (travelling verbs) are those which express the action of the subject *on* the object—as in 'He greeted me.' The verb 'greeted' is said to be in its active role or voice. And from your study of verb-forms, you know that this action is *simple* rather than continuing.

Now, if we turn the sentence around—'I was greeted by him'—the direction of travel is reversed. The verb 'was greeted' is now carrying action *from* the object *to* the subject. When a verb reverses its action in this way, it is said to be in its *passive* role (or voice).

Let us turn a few more sentences around just for the practice: 'I am donating ten shillings'—'Ten shillings is (or *are*) being donated by me;' 'I will judge the dogs'—'The dogs will be judged by me.' 'The baby ate the candle'—'The candle was eaten by the baby.'

Notice how the passive role is formed in each case. Aside from minor changes in the normal verb-form, each verb has added a verb-helper—and all of these helpers are the verb 'be' or *forms* of it: *was, being, are, is.* Another important point to notice is that when the verb is passive, the object takes the form of a phrase—'by him', 'by me', 'by the baby'.

Only those verbs which take an *object* can be made passive. It stands to reason that there must *be* an object in order for it to express action *upon* the subject. And because verbs take objects *only* when they are used transitively, a verb used *in*transitively cannot be made passive: e.g. 'He works here'—'here' is an adverb telling *where* he works, so there is no object which can act upon the subject; we cannot say 'Here is worked by him.' Similarly, linking verbs cannot be used passively: e.g. 'She is nine years old'—again there is no object to act upon the subject—'Nine years old is been by she,' doesn't make much sense.

A final point: Do not confuse the transitive or intransitive nature of a verb with its ability to express simple or continuing action. Even though a verb may not be able to have an object, it is still capable of expressing both simple and continuing action: e.g. 'The house is old'—a linking verb expressing simple action or state of being; 'The house is becoming old,' expresses a continuing or progressive state of being.

Try your hand at reversing these sentences: 'I bought the flowers;' 'She lent the picture;' 'He dropped the chandelier;' 'Lightning struck the tree;' 'A diamond drill dug the shaft;' 'Paramount made the film;' 'A new girl typed the letters.'

For many of the verb-forms you have learned, having simple and continuing action, there is a corresponding passive form. Compare the following list with that on page 27.

SIMPLE		CONTINUING
He is seen	PRESENT	He is being seen
He was seen	PAST	He was being seen
He will be seen	FUTURE	He will be being seen
He has been seen	PRESENT COMPLETED	
He had been seen	PAST COMPLETED	no form
He will have been seen	FUTURE COMPLETED	

The future continuing form sees little use; in most situations its meaning is adequately expressed by the future simple; i.e. 'He will be interviewed on television,' rather than 'He will be being interviewed on television.'

Some of the verbs in the following exercise are active, some are passive. Name each italicised verb, telling its person, number, time, action (simple or continuing) and its voice (active or passive).

EXAMPLES: 1: This extraordinary picture *was painted* by an ape. [(picture) was painted—3rd person, singular, past, simple, passive voice]. 2: *Could* I *see* your television licence, please? [(I) (could—helper) see—1st person, singular present, simple, active voice]. **(Answers: page 61.)**

1. Raw sienna *is called* an earth colour. 2. They *will be having* their supper soon. 3. Uranus *can* barely *be seen* by the naked eye. 4. We *had been carried* ten miles in a dugout canoe. 5. Canal travel *was introduced* into Britain by the Romans. 6. For sixpence, a newspaper *provides* the same amount of reading as a novel. 7. The earliest known dam *was built* in 2750 B.C. in Egypt. 8. The ship *will be named* 'Ibida'. 9. The car *is being re-painted.*

Mood

Verbs are said to have 'mood'. As used in grammar, however, this word means little more than 'manner'. There are three moods: **indicating mood,** the **command mood** and the **supposing mood.**

Indicating mood

The *indicating mood* (traditionally called the **indicative** mood) refers to verbs as they are used in the everyday give-and-take conversation, i.e. questions and answers— 'Where is the boy who looks after the sheep?' 'It's his day off.'

Command mood

Verbs used in command-type sentences are said to be in the mood of command (traditionally, the **imperative** mood). 'Bring my pipe, my bowl and two or three fiddlers,' 'Don't drop your ash on the carpet!' 'Stand at ease!' The command mood is also that of signs: 'Keep to the left,' 'Dead slow.'

Supposing mood

The *supposing mood* (traditionally, the **subjunctive** mood) is used for wishes—'I wish I were in Spain now;' for hopes—'May you both be very happy;' for uncertain conditions—'She looks as though she were ill;' for untrue conditions—'If he were here now . . .;' for impossible conditions—'If I were you, I'd . . .'

The verb-forms you have learned up to this point, both active and passive, have been in the *indicating mood.* The mood of command has only two verb-forms; for the verb 'see', they are 'see' and 'be seen': e.g. '(You) See that this mess is cleaned up quickly,' '(You) Stand up, Jones, and be seen!'

The verb-forms for the *supposing mood* are the same for all verbs (but one) as the indicating mood, except for a small change for 3rd person singular, present time—'If he have faith, he need not fear' (*have* instead of *has*); 'Should she find this, we'd be doomed,' (*find* instead of *finds*). However, the verb 'be' requires several changes for the *supposing mood.* The following table shows the differences between the two moods. The word 'if' is shown because it so often introduces the supposing situation—'If I were she,' 'If you be he,' and etc.

PRESENT INDICATING		*verb 'be'*	**PRESENT SUPPOSING**	
I am	he is		(if) I be	(if) he be
we are	they are		(if) we be	(if) they be
you are			(if) you be	
PAST INDICATING			**PAST SUPPOSING**	
I was	he was		(if) I were	(if) he were
we were	they were		(if) we were	(if) they were
you were			(if) you were	

PRESENT INDICATING		*verb 'see'*	**PRESENT SUPPOSING**	
I see	he sees		(if) I see	(if) he see
we see	they see		(if) we see	(if) they see
you see			(if) you see	

As the table shows, all forms of the *present* supposing mood of 'be' are different from the indicating mood. In the *past* supposing mood, there are just two changes—for first person singular and third person singular. For all other verbs, the verb 'see' being representative, the only change is in the third person singular of the present time.

The use of 'be' is well-rooted in many stock expressions: *If that be true, So be it, Patience be damned, Be she victorious, happy and glorious, Far be it from me to judge, Be that as it may, If the facts be known. Be* is still used in formal speech: 'It is thought fitting that the matter be discussed at an executive level,' 'I move that a committee be formed to study the matter;' though we tend now to insert the word 'should' or perhaps rearrange the sentence to eliminate 'be'; e.g. 'The pilot suggests the route be altered.' = 'The pilot suggests altering the route.'

The use of 'were' can be confusing unless we realise that the *past supposing time* is not really a time at all; it has nothing to do with 'pastness'. Consider the use of 'was' and 'were' in these two sentences: 'If he *was* at the party last night, I didn't see him.' 'If he *were* here now he could tell us if he *was* at the party.' Where 'was' is used, it refers to an event that actually happened in the past. On the other hand 'were' refers to nothing in the past; it merely tells us he is *not* here; and if, by some magical power, he could be produced instantly, he would be able to answer a question.

By this you will see that 'were' does not automatically follow 'if'. Two conditions are necessary for the use of 'were'—a *supposing* situation, and *no* past happening. Compare the following:

> 'If this *were* my car, I'd scrap it,' 'If your car *was* hit yesterday, it isn't noticeable.' 'If he *were* healthy, he'd be able to work,' 'If he *was* healthy last week, he certainly isn't healthy today.' 'If she *were* a good skier, we'd take our holiday in Switzerland,' 'If she *was* a good skier last year, she has forgotten a great deal now.'

In the first sentence of each pair, there is no 'pastness'. Also, these sentences begin with an untrue condition: 'If this were my car' means it *isn't* my car. 'If he were healthy' means he *isn't* healthy. 'If she were a good skier' means she *isn't* a good skier. However, the second sentence in each pair has genuine 'pastness'; more, the speaker is at least willing to *believe* the 'if-condition'—'If your car was hit yesterday (and I'm willing to believe you when you say it *was* hit), it isn't noticeable,' 'If he was healthy last week (and I'm willing to believe this by what you have said about him), he certainly isn't healthy today,' 'If she was a good skier last year (and I believe this by what I have heard), she has forgotten a great deal now.'

Briefly, use 'were' for any untrue or impossible condition, i.e. *If I were you; if I were king; if he were taller; if she were a film star;* and use 'was' for a past event you are willing to accept as true, i.e. *If it was her birthday yesterday, then . . ., If she was Miss England of* 1932, *then . . ., If he was the top boy in his class last term, then . . .*

Obviously, we need never worry about the correctness of 'was' or 'were' for *you, we, they;* the forms are the same for *indicating* and *supposing:* e.g. 'If you were a better swimmer, we could try the deeper water,' 'If they were in London last week, they didn't call.' We need not puzzle here whether the mood is indicating or supposing because there is only one way to express both.

The word 'if' is not necessary to introduce a supposing condition; it can be done equally well by expressions such as *imagine . . . just suppose . . . as though.* Which of the following examples are right and which are wrong? (**Answers: page 61.**)

1. You'd think he was a monkey the way he jumps around.

2. Better she were dead than know this. 3. To hear him tell it, you'd think I was a magician. 4. As a matter of fact, I was a magician at one time. 5. I wish I were twins at a time like this. 6. If this bar was stronger, I'd show you how I used to do somersaults. 7. If the car was waxed, they did a poor job. 8. Supposing it was Mother who telephoned last night. 9. If it was for me to say, I'd drop the charge.

Part Three

MORE ABOUT SUBJECTS

A SENTENCE may have more than one subject: e.g. 'I, you and Pancho should ride to Abilene.' Here, there are three subjects: *I* and *you* and *Pancho*. This is a multiple subject. But sometimes there are two subjects equalling only one: e.g. 'Frank, my friend, smashed my motorbike.' Here, 'Frank' and 'friend' indicate the same person. They are said to be **appositive** though 'in tandem' might be more descriptive.

Agreement of subject and verb

The subject of a sentence must agree in number with its verb; that is, both must be singular, or both must be plural. There is little chance of confusion when working with the personal pronouns—I, you, we, they *have*; he, she (and 'it') *has*; but the choice is rarely so simple. Here are some general rules to help you in making your decisions.

A double subject joined by 'and' requires a plural verb

WRONG: Design and construction is equally important. (are)

WRONG: John and Mary considers the house too large. (consider)

Note: When two words have, by association, become accepted as a single thought, a singular verb may be used: e.g. Fish and chips *is* a good cheap meal. The salt and pepper *is* on the table. A double subject preceded by 'every' is singular: e.g. Every man and woman wants (not *want*) security in their old age.

Verbs do not agree with the object or with words in the predicate

WRONG: The important thing to notice are the many varieties of car design. (*thing* is the subject; verb should be *is*)

'Here' and 'there' cannot be the subjects of a sentence

Even though these words may appear at the beginning of a sentence, they are **adverbs of place**; and though the verb usually follows them, it must agree with the *subject*.

WRONG: Here's the tickets for your parcels. ('s = is)

Sentence re-arrangement quickly shows the error: The tickets for your parcels *are* here.

A prepositional phrase following the subject does not alter the number of the verb

WRONG: The decision of labour representatives to hold general meetings every four months seem a major step toward better understanding with the company. (*decision* is the subject; verb should be *seems*)

WRONG: The difference between the boys' and girls' marks are to be discussed. (*difference* is the subject; verb should be *is*)

Singular pronouns and adjectives require singular verbs

The following words require that a singular verb be used, regardless of whether they are the noun-subject or adjectives *describing* the noun-subject: *one, each, everyone, everybody, anyone, anybody, someone, somebody, no one, another, either, neither.*

First, consider them as nouns:

WRONG: One of the ships have been sunk. ('one' is the subject; one *has* been sunk)

WRONG: Each of the children play some instrument well. (plays)

WRONG: Everyone concerned with personal freedom are watching the court's decision. (is)

WRONG: Neither of the political parties show much dynamic thinking. (shows)

Note: the pronoun 'none' may be singular or plural depending on whether it is referring to a quantity or to a number: e.g. 'Have we any beer? No, there *is* none. Have we any eggs? No, there *are* none.'

Now consider them as adjectives:—

WRONG: Each type have different qualities. (has)

WRONG: Neither person were telling the truth. (was)

Words joined to a subject by 'with', 'in addition to', 'as well as', 'including', 'not to omit', 'plus' and similar expressions, do not affect the verb

WRONG: The farm, including cattle, poultry, feed and crops were insured. (*farm* is the singular subject; verb should be *was*)

WRONG: The tree as well as the shrubs around it were beginning to die. (was)

A collective noun takes a singular verb if it is thought of as a whole, but a plural verb if its parts are being considered

RIGHT: The fleet is lying at anchor.

RIGHT: The fleet are composed of warships, cruisers and submarines.

Nouns, plural in form, but singular in meaning, take a singular verb

The following nouns take a singular verb: *measles, mathematics, news, summons, mumps.*

RIGHT: Mumps for an older person is more than a mere inconvenience.

There are no definite rules for many other words, i.e. *ethics, politics, physics.* It cannot be considered wrong to use either a singular or plural verb.

Plural subjects describing a unit of measurement are considered singular

RIGHT: Ten miles is a long way to ski.

RIGHT: Five thousand tons is the largest recorded cargo for this ship.

The word 'number' is plural when it means 'many' and singular when it refers to a mathematical figure

WRONG: A number of fish is washed up every day onto the beach. (are)

RIGHT: A number is painted on the underside of every chair.

If two subjects are joined by 'either–or' or 'neither–nor,' the verb agrees with the subject nearer it

RIGHT: Neither the committee members nor the chairman *has* left.

RIGHT: Either the baby or the dogs *have* taken the glove.

If one subject is used affirmatively and the other negatively, the verb agrees with the subject used affirmatively

RIGHT: The canary, not the cats, *is* the nuisance.

MORE ABOUT OBJECTS

The object of a sentence answers What or Whom after a transitive verb. The object can be double or multiple in form: e.g. He read biographies, novels and poems in his spare time. *Biographies, novels* and *poems* are equal objects to the verb 'read'. Objects can also be appositive—in tandem: e.g. Everyone liked Mr. Cargill, the postman.

Indirect Objects

Sometimes a verb has two objects of which one is clearly more important than the other. Consider the sentence, 'He read stories to his children.' There are two objects: 'stories' and 'children'. Which is the more important of the two? Logically, he read stories, and his children benefited from it—'Children' might be thought to receive action as a consequence of 'reading *stories*'—they received the action indirectly, you might say. 'Stories' then is the main thing 'he' read; it is called the **direct object.** 'Children', the secondary object, is called the **indirect object.**

Normally, we would write this sentence, 'He read his children stories.' Here, the indirect object is placed ahead of the direct object. This is usual. We say the preposition 'for' or 'to' is *understood* with indirect objects. In other words, we take 'for' or 'to' for granted: e.g. He read (to) his children stories.

The distinction between direct and indirect objects is clearer in this sentence, 'He gave his wife a box of chocolates.' What did he give? His wife? No, he gave a box of chocolates—and his wife benefited from it. Of course the word 'benefited' becomes suspect in a sentence like, 'He kicked him in the head;' but the position of the objects is in no way changed. This is the general rule; indirect objects usually *follow* the verb and *precede* the direct object.

The following sentence should not be confused with what has been covered: 'They elected him shop-steward.' 'Him' and 'shop-steward' are *not* direct and indirect objects, nor are they objects in tandem (apposite). They represent an elliptical (condensed) form of 'They elected him *to be* shop-steward.' This form will be covered later.

Here is how double subjects, double objects and indirect objects can be shown in graphic analysis—'Gerald and Martha taught him to sing and (to) dance.'

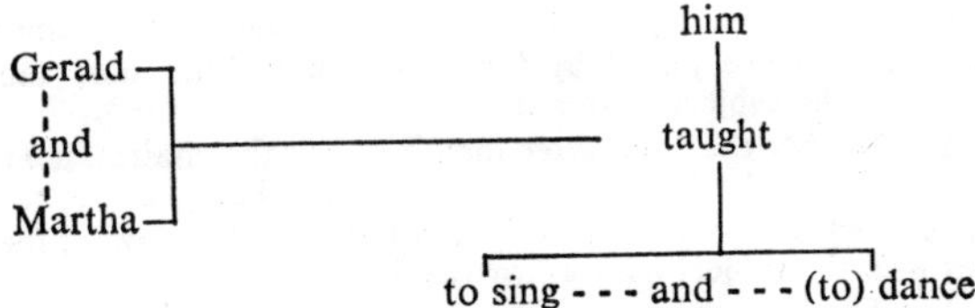

As you see, the indirect object is placed directly *above* the verb, and the direct object has been separated. In another: She took them fresh fruit and a cut of meat.

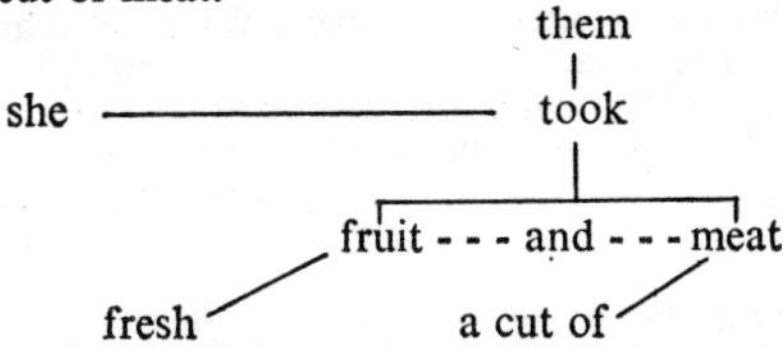

Commit the following sentences to diagram form. As you finish each, check the result against those on page 61:—

1. The butcher gave the dog a bone. 2. Give me a needle and thread. 3. The postman brought you a packet and two letters this morning. 4. Don't give the baby buttons. 5. The prices of fish and meat give one a shock. 6. The corvette and the submarine collided off Portsmouth.

Part Four

VERBS OF UNLIMITED USE

Participle

WE CAN SAY 'He *has* a red nose,' but we cannot say 'I *has* a red nose.' For this reason we say the verb-form 'has' is of limited use. It is limited in its use to third person singular. Again, we can say 'It is cold,' but we cannot say 'It is cold yesterday;' so the verb-form 'is' also has limited use—limited in this situation by time. All verbs in their simplest forms are limited in this way; *go, goes, went, shall go, see, sees, saw, will see*—all simple present, past and future verb-forms are limited in their use.

Now consider the *second* part of the combination verbs in these three sentences: 'They were *singing* a carol;' 'He is *singing* a carol;' 'We shall be *singing* a carol.' Though the time and person changes in each sentence, the verb-form 'singing' remains the same. A verb-form that remains the same under varying conditions is said to be *unlimited* in its use; or stated traditionally, it has *infinite* use.

The word 'singing' is called a **participle.** Participles have three forms; one form, the **present participle,** always ends with *-ing*: e.g. *standing, running, jumping, loving, going, seeing.* Participles have two jobs—one, as you have seen, gives the continuing-action form to a verb: 'He was singing off-key.' But what is it doing in this sentence, 'He needs a singing lesson'? Here, 'singing' has nothing to do with the action of the verb 'needs'; it is telling us something about the noun 'lesson'; it is, in fact, an adjective. And that is the *second* role of a participle.

Participles, then, can either form part of a combination verb—to give a continuing action to the verb—or else they can work as adjectives. Here are a few examples of present participles in the role of adjectives: *howling wind, running seas, screaming sirens, standing order, leading question, jumping bean, vanishing cream, rolling stone, tiring trip.*

There are two other types of participles—the **past participle** and the **complete** or **perfect participle.** While all present participles end with *-ing*, the *past* and *complete participles* end in different ways, depending on the nature of the verb.

The past *time* for the simple verb 'sing' is 'sang'—they are both limited or finite in their use—we cannot say 'I sang tomorrow,' or 'I sing yesterday.' The verb-form 'sung,' however, is unlimited or infinite; it can be used for all persons and for all times: e.g. 'I had sung it,' 'They will have sung it.' But even when it is used in the future, as it is in the second sentence, it has a quality of *pastness*, hasn't it? 'Sung' is, in fact, called the *past participle*. Can it be used as an adjective? Yes—'It was a well-sung song.'

The past *participles* of some verbs are different in form from the past *time* of the verb; with other verbs, both forms are the same. Compare the following.

SIMPLE PRESENT TIME	SIMPLE PAST TIME	PAST PARTICIPLE
break	broke	broken
eat	ate	eaten
rent	rented	rented
test	tested	tested
forget	forgot	forgotten
bite	bit	bitten
help	helped	helped
drive	drove	driven
see	saw	seen
walk	walked	walked

Past participles cannot be used as simple verbs are, though you may have heard 'I done it,' or 'I seen it.' Nor can simple verb forms be used as adjectives, though again, you may have heard of a 'half-ate cake.' Whenever you want to recall the past participle form of a verb, begin a sentence with 'I have . . . *eaten, rented, tested, forgotten, bitten,* and etc.

Examples of past participles performing as adjectives are: ***trained nurse, broken promise, tired feet, burnt toast, lost property, dehydrated milk, wrinkled skin, exposed film, rusted bolt, worn path, ploughed field, tested recipe.***

The third and last form participles can take is the *complete* or *perfect* participle. It is formed by adding 'having' to the past participle, thus, *having seen, having broken, having tried, having driven.* The complete participle is an adjective: 'Having left, the train could be heard whistling in the valley.' 'Having left' describes the train; a suitable one-word equivalent might be 'departed'—'The *departed* train could be heard whistling in the valley.' Another: 'The gun, having fired, was too hot to handle.' A suitable one-word equivalent would be 'discharged'—'The *discharged* gun was too hot to handle.'

The following table shows the relationship between the three participles:

	Active	**Passive**
present	singing	being sung
past	—	sung
complete	having sung	having been sung

The past participle is **passive.** We can test this by trying it in a sentence: 'The hymn was sung by a choir.' It produces a typically passive sentence. This is the only way 'sung' can be used in a sentence; it cannot be used as an active verb—'I sung a song'—this is incorrect for 'I sang a song.' Similarly, the *complete participle* cannot take the place of a verb in a sentence. It is unlimited or infinite in its use. For it to be suitable for verb duty, it need be made limited. This is done by using limited forms of 'having'.

have seen	had seen	shall have seen
have broken	had broken	shall have broken
have driven	had driven	shall have driven

This is no different from the material you learned earlier in 3rd person form—'he has seen,' 'he had seen,' and 'he will have seen.'

Infinitives

You have learned of finite or limited verbs (see, sees, saw) and infinite or unlimited verbs (seeing, seen, having seen). Participles are *one* kind of infinite verb; there are two others—the **infinitive** and the **gerund.** The name *infinitive* is misleading; an infinitive is no more *infinite* than a participle or a gerund; however, the name is firmly anchored in traditional usage so it will be used here.

An *infinitive* is the role of a finite verb in an infinite manner. Infinitives more often appear composed of two words: e.g. *to find, to see, to know.* Infinitives are used as nouns, adjective or adverbs; they *never* join with or form part of the verb of the sentence—even though they might be situated next to it: e.g. 'I would like to see Mr. Smith.' The verb is *not* 'would like to see'—it is 'would like'; 'to see' is introducing an infinitive phrase, object to the verb. Here are examples of infinitives acting as nouns, adjectives and adverbs. Where possible, one-word equivalents are given to help explain the infinitive's role.

noun To err is human. (*to err*—noun-subject = *error*)
I like to travel. (*to travel*—noun-object = *change*)

adjective He is the man to watch. (*to watch* = *interesting* or *suspected*)
We have no time to wait. (*to wait* = *extra* or *spare*)

adverb He was glad to have come. (*to have come*—describes adjective *glad*)
She is delightful to watch. (*to watch*—describes adjective *delightful*)

Puzzle: Why is the word 'to' omitted from the second, fourth and sixth sentences?

1. I taught her to dance. 2. I saw her dance. 3. I wanted him to sing. 4. I heard him sing. 5. We asked them to go. 6. We watched them go.

Answer: There is no logical reason. Through accepted usage, certain verbs such as *see, hear, need, know, observe, let, watch, feel* require that the 'to' be dropped from the infinitives that follow them. The absence of the 'to' does not diminish their role as infinitives, though it makes them more difficult to spot.

Sometimes there is a choice of including the 'to' or omitting it: e.g. 'Help me to pack,' 'Help me pack.' The omission of words is a common occurrence in English; it is called **ellipsis**—though this means no more than 'omission'. More will be said of ellipsis later.

The complete (perfect) infinitives—*to have done, to have seen, to have been*—have a quality of imagination about them: e.g. *To have administered the drug would have been dangerous.* In other words, the drug was *not* administered; the statement merely imagines or supposes the outcome if such-and-such had been carried out.

Gerunds

Gerunds are as easy to spot as present participles; they are, in fact, identical in appearance—*skiing, swimming, jumping, running.* The difficulty lies in telling which is a gerund and which is a participle. The answer depends on the job being done. Participles are *adjectives*; gerunds are *nouns.* Traditional teaching stressed the different origins of the participle and gerund; but this tends to cloud the issue. It is much simpler to think of a gerund as being a 'participle acting as a noun'. Here are gerunds in use.

Skiing is fun—'skiing'—noun, subject of the sentence.
She likes wrestling—'wrestling'—noun, object of verb *likes*
It is too shallow for swimming—'swimming'—noun, object of preposition *for*

There is small chance of confusion here; a participle (an adjective) could not fill these three jobs.

Like nouns, a gerund can be plural: *sightings, meetings, happenings, awakenings.* You will recall that nouns were sometimes used to describe other nouns as in 'apple tree'. This will provide a clue to help you determine the difference between the following two columns of words.

surprising sight	knitting needles
penetrating glance	modelling school
puzzling riddle	juggling act
charming conversation	boxing career

The left-hand column consists of *participles* and nouns. The right-hand column consists of *gerunds* being used to describe nouns. How can you tell the difference? On the right we have 'needles *for* knitting', 'school *for* modelling', 'act *of* juggling', and 'career *of* boxing'. Both words in each expression are nouns; whereas the *-ing* words in the left column are rarely thought of as being nouns —though of course they *could* play this role: e.g. *Puzzling is the magician's livelihood*—meaning the magician earns a living by puzzling people.

The unlimited or infinite verb-forms are called **verbals** to distinguish them from the ordinary limited or finite verbs (see, sees, saw). Here are the verbals you have now learned, expressing the verb 'go'.

Infinitives

present *to go*—noun, adverb, adjective
complete *to have gone*—noun, adverb, adjective

Gerund	*going*—noun	
Participles—*active*		*passive*
present	*going*—verb-form for continuing action or adjective	*being gone*—adjective
past	—	*gone*—verb-form for completed action or adjective
complete	*having gone*—adjective	*having been gone*—adjective

Verbal phrases

All the phrases you learned earlier began with a preposition: e.g. *under the bed, by me, in the river, for him.* They are called prepositional phrases. Prepositional phrases always have either a noun or pronoun for an object.

Verbal phrases, i.e. phrases beginning with a participle, infinitive or gerund, may have a noun or pronoun object, or they may instead have only an adverb—or indeed, they may have both at once. Here are examples using the present, past and complete participles, the infinitive, and the gerund.

Firing blindly, he heard one of his pursuers cry out. 'He' is the only word in the sentence which the present participle 'firing' could logically describe. 'Firing' is, in turn, described by the adverb 'blindly'. Together they form a present participle phrase describing 'he'.

Driven relentlessly, he began to ascend the glacier. The past participle 'driven' describes 'he'. The adverb 'relentlessly' describes 'driven'. They form a past participle phrase describing 'he'.

Having spoken abruptly, she blushed and left the room. 'Having spoken,' the complete participle, describes 'she'; it is described in turn by the adverb 'abruptly'. 'Having spoken abruptly' is a complete participle phrase describing 'she'.

This is no time to walk slowly. 'To walk' tells us time-for-what?—it describes 'time'. 'Slowly' is an adverb describing 'to walk'. 'To walk slowly' is an infinitive phrase acting as an adjective to describe 'time'. This analysis might be clearer if the sentence were changed: *This is no time for walking slowly.* Here, 'walking' is a gerund, a noun-object to the preposition 'for'. 'For walking' describes 'time' in the same way 'to walk' did. Switching from infinitive to gerund in this way often shows a relationship more clearly.

To have refused might have been dangerous. Here, the complete or perfect infinitive 'to have refused' is the subject of the sentence.

Living dangerously can be fun. The gerund 'living' is noun-subject of the sentence; 'dangerously' is an adverb. Gerunds are usually followed by an *adverb,* or preceded by an *adjective,* i.e. though we wouldn't say 'living dangerous, we *would* say 'dangerous living'—again, 'mad living', but 'living madly'.

Phrases such as those above are often lengthened by the addition of a prepositional phrase: e.g. **Firing blindly through the bush,**

he . . .; Driven relentlessly by cold and hunger, he . . .; Having spoken abruptly in front of the guests, she . . .; This is no time to walk slowly through the woods; Living dangerously at times, can be fun. The prepositional phrase becomes *part* of the verbal phrase.

Again, verbals can simply take an object: e.g. **Firing six quick shots, he . . .; Driven ten bitter miles, he . . .; Having spoken nonsense, she . . .**

Tell him to mind his own business. 'To mind' plus the noun 'business' plus two adjectives form an infinitive phrase, object of 'tell'—'him' being the indirect object.

What does she hope to find? 'What' is the pronoun *object* of 'to find'—'She does hope to find what.' 'To find what' is the object of 'does hope'.

Sometimes verbals are immediately followed by a prepositional phrase: e.g. **Firing over the ridge, he . . .; Driven by hunger and cold, he . . .; Having spoken for the younger generation, she . . .** These are all participle phrases.

He saw a ship *heading toward him.* A present participle phrase—one-word equivalent, 'approaching'—an *approaching ship.*

They saw a large oval face *covered with hair.* A past participle phrase—one-word equivalent, 'bearded'.

To work by torchlight **proved more dangerous than he expected.** The infinitive phrase 'to work by torchlight' is the subject of the sentence.

He decided *to surface under the ship's hull.* 'To surface under the ship's hull' is an infinitive phrase, object to the verb 'decided'.

She heard the choir *singing a hymn.* A present participle phrase—one-word equivalent, 'harmonising.' But now consider, 'She heard the choir *sing* a hymn.' 'Sing' in this sentence might be mistaken for a finite verb (sing, sings, sang) if we didn't remember that 'hear' is one of the verbs requiring the omission of 'to' from any infinitive which follows it. 'Sing,' then, is here an infinitive; 'sing a hymn' may or may not be considered a describer of 'choir'. What is the alternative?

Consider this sentence: 'We asked him to play the cello.' Is 'him' the *indirect* object and 'to play the cello' the *direct* object? Omitting 'him', 'We asked to play the cello,' conveys an entirely different meaning from what was intended. Instead, could 'him' be the direct object with 'to play the cello' as an infinitive describer? The equivalent of 'to play the cello' would be 'cello-playing'. 'We asked cello-playing him.' If this makes sense, it is certainly not near the *intended* sense of the original sentence.

In a situation such as this—and this is peculiar to infinitives—the infinitive is considered to have taken a subject—'him'—and 'him to play the cello' is the infinitive phrase, object to the verb 'asked'. The rule governing this novelty states that both the subject *and* the object of an infinitive must be in the *objective* case; thus, we have, 'They asked *me to meet her*;' 'They told *him to see me*;' 'We watched *her take him.*' All of the personal pronouns here are in the objective case; each of the italicised groups, consisting of subject, infinitive and object, is the object of the sentence.

Ellipsis (omission) can obscure this relationship: e.g. 'They elected him shop-steward.' The complete sense is 'They elected him *to be* shop-steward;' 'him shop-steward' then is an abbreviated infinitive phrase, object of 'elected'.

Sometimes a verbal phrase is preceded by a preposition: e.g. 'He is *about* to leave soon.' Here, the infinitive phrase 'to leave soon' is considered to be the noun-object of the preposition—or the equivalent of 'He is about leaving.' Two more examples: 'He stayed *after* hearing the news,' '*By* having told the truth, he escaped heavy penalty.'

Unrelated, unattached or dangling participles

Participles are adjectives; participle *phrases* must *also* be adjectives. To be an adjective phrase though, there must be a noun or pronoun for the adjective or participle to describe. Sometimes people forget to include the noun; when this occurs, the participle is said to be unattached or dangling e.g., 'Throwing several stones, the squirrels sped away.' The only word for the participle to describe is 'squirrels'. For this sentence to be correct as it stands, the squirrels would have had to throw stones before running away. This is not the intended meaning, of course, and so a *person* must be mentioned. 'Throwing several stones, he watched the squirrels speed away.'

Sometimes the noun or pronoun is included in the sentence, but placed too far from the participle: e.g. 'Offering lumps of sugar, the horse walked calmly toward her.' Again, the horse would appear to be offering lumps of sugar. Misunderstandings of this sort are avoided by placing the noun or pronoun immediately before or immediately after the participle phrase—'Offering lumps of sugar, she enticed the horse slowly toward her.'

Absolute phrase

The misunderstanding discussed above cannot happen in an absolute phrase because the noun or pronoun described *by* the participle is contained *in* the phrase: e.g. 'The sky having cleared, we all went home.' Here, 'sky', the noun described by the complete participle, is part of the phrase. 'The sky having cleared' is considered to be absolute or independent of the rest of the sentence—a small self-contained expression that creates a setting for the main part of the sentence 'we all went home.' As you see, the requirements of an absolute phrase are: 1. that it contain a verbal, 2. that it include the noun or pronoun described *by* the verbal. Other examples: *All things being equal, we'll go by train; Weather permitting, he will sail on Sunday; That being the case, I'll detain you no longer.*

The following three sentences show how similar material would be presented using a complete participle in 1. a participle phrase, 2. a dangling participle phrase, 3. an absolute phrase.

Having rested, the troops continued the march.
Having rested, the march was continued.
The troops having rested, the march was continued.

Through usage, certain participles may sometimes work as prepositions; they are: *concerning, considering, pending, owing to, failing*. When these words are used as prepositions, they cannot be regarded as dangling or unrelated participles, as in: 'Considering the trouble, the job yielded small profit.' Here, 'considering the trouble' is a sort of absolute comment equal to 'in my opinion'. It does not *need* attachment to the main part of the sentence.

However, if 'considering' is used as a *participle*, it must then be related to a noun or pronoun, as it is in: 'Considering every possible escape, he tried the windows,' and not left dangling as in: 'Considering every possible escape, the windows were found to be barred.'

Describing and commenting phrases

Consider the difference in meaning between these two sentences:

A—The boys wearing short pants felt cold.
B—The boys, wearing short pants, felt cold.

Sentence A would have us believe that of *all* the boys present, those wearing short pants felt cold. 'Wearing short pants' limits *by description* the boys being discussed.

Sentence B would have us believe that *all* the boys were wearing short pants, and *all* of them felt cold. The sentence could also be written, 'The boys (wearing short pants) felt cold.' 'Wearing short pants' is a general comment about *all* of the boys present.

Traditionally, the distinction between these two phrases is termed **limiting** or **non-limiting; defining** or **non-defining; restrictive** or **non-restrictive**; however 'describing' and 'commenting' express this difference just as well in familiar terms. The phrase in sentence A describes the *particular* boys being discussed; the phrase in sentence B merely makes a casual comment—almost an aside—about *all* of the boys.

As you see, the *intent* of a phrase can be changed by the inclusion or omission of commas. The point is raised here because it can have great bearing on the material just covered. Consider the difference between these two sentences.

The dogs having been fed, we sat down and rested.
The dogs, having been fed, sat down and rested.

The phrase in the first sentence is absolute; it has no grammatical link with the subject of the sentence 'we' nor with any other word in the main part of the sentence. This is the normal relationship for an absolute construction. In the second sentence, however, 'having been fed' is a complete or perfect participle (in passive form) describing the subject of the sentence, 'dogs'. Both sentences are correct for the meanings they intend to express.

But if a comma is placed after 'dogs' in the first sentence, we would have nonsense. This will serve to remind you that absolute constructions should *not* have commas within their phrases.

On the other hand, if the comma following 'dogs' in the second sentence were removed, the comma following 'fed' would also have to be removed to make sense—The dogs having been fed sat down and rested. But now we have a sentence with a different meaning; the sentence implies that there are other *un*fed dogs still standing.

The split infinitive

For many years it was thought wrong to split an infinitive, but now grammarians are trying to find who started the mischief. To split an infinitive, simply place a word between the two parts of the infinitive (if it *has* two parts): e.g. to *briefly try*. Here, an adverb has been inserted between 'to' and 'try', the two parts of the infinitive. Splitting the infinitive in this way is often the sanest and most pleasant-sounding way to express a thought: e.g. 'He failed to completely understand what was being said to him.' In this sentence it might be further argued that the same sense could not be conveyed *without* splitting the infinitive. H. F. Fowler says, in the *Dictionary of Modern English Usage*, 'We will split infinitives sooner than be ambiguous or artificial.' Few would argue with Fowler on this point.

Picking out phrases and identifying them correctly is not an easy matter—far from it. You are advised to re-read Part Four at least once more before proceeding with the following puzzles.

In the following twenty sentences there are a total of thirty-four phrases to be identified. Pick out each phrase; determine what kind it is, and what word, if any, it describes. Check the answer for each sentence on page 62 before moving on to the next.

1. They wanted to see the king. 2. Girls wearing smart white tunics met the train. 3. The train having left, we waited for another. 4. He shouted a muffled answer through the window. 5. Having finished the letters, she went home. 6. Silver birches will grow in even the poorest soil. 7. Having been timed flying at 200 mph, the swift is probably the fastest bird in the world. 8. The use of the Mach scale for aircraft speeds was introduced by Professor Acherer of Zurich. 9. All things considered, a cruiser is just a fast, light battleship. 10. To find the area of a circle we need first to know its radius. 11. We want to toast the chestnuts. 12. Reading a book takes time. 13. Feeling sorry for yourself will not help matters. 14. You've ruined these shoes by wading in puddles. 15. Tired of saving money, buying a car was put off. 16. There wasn't much beer, shared between the eight. 17. I want you to find this man at all costs. 18. Help having finally arrived, he sat down and wept. 19. Having tried every other means, he began battering the door with a log. 20. Dashed against rocks by the seething rollers, Meredith staggered onto the beach.

Part Five

YOU HAVE COVERED six of the eight parts of speech: noun, pronoun, verb, adjective, adverb and preposition. There remain but two other parts of speech. One is simple, the **interjection.**

INTERJECTION

Interjections can be grunts, groans, gasps of surprise or a proper word, as in 'My! You are becoming a big girl, aren't you?' 'O where O where has my little lamb gone?' 'Good heavens! I think I've lost my purse.' An interjection has no grammatical relationship with the other words in a sentence.

CONJUNCTION

DEFINITION: **A conjunction joins words or groups of words together. The most common conjunction is 'and'. Other conjunctions are:** ***but, for, either/or, neither/nor, whether, if, that, who, which, where, when, why, since, because, although, while, however, moreover, nevertheless, therefore.***

Some conjunctions can be used to join single words or groups of words: e.g. 'Jack *and* Jill went up the hill;' 'Jack went up the hill *and* Jill went up the hill;' 'Fred *or* John will be here soon;' 'Fred will be here soon *or* John will be here soon.' Other conjunctions join only *groups* of words: 'He didn't win *although* he should have.'

We will concern ourselves here with conjunctions that join certain *groups* of words together, or **clauses** as they are called.

CLAUSE

DEFINITION: **A clause is a group of words containing a subject and a finite verb.**

A clause is simply a *part* of a sentence. The difference between a clause and a sentence is sometimes slight: e.g. 'I am going,' is a sentence, but in 'I am going and you are staying,' the same group of words is called a clause.—'I am going,' is now only a *part* of the sentence.

Clauses are said to be either independent or dependent. An independent clause makes complete sense by itself, a dependent clause doesn't. Here are some independent clauses:—

I swim *and* she plays tennis = I swim. She plays tennis.
I read *but* she writes = I read. She writes.
I will read *or* she will write = I will read. She will write.

The conjunctions *and, but, or* are the most common ones used for joining independent clauses together. Now look at some sentences containing one independent clause and one dependent clause.

She'll be unhappy *if* you don't come.	Dep. clause: (if) you don't come.
I don't know *whether* I will see him.	Dep. clause: (whether) I will see him.
This is the plan *that* he drew.	Dep. clause: (that) he drew.

It might be argued that if the three conjunctions *if, whether* and *that* were to be detached from the clauses in the same way *and, but* and *or* were in the earlier three sentences, the resultant clauses— would be equally independent. That is true—they *would* be independent; however, it is the character or nature *of* these later conjunctions which *make* the clauses dependent. That is to say, the nature of the conjunction 'if' is such as to introduce an adverbial clause of condition or reason, which in turn, is going to limit the verb in the main clause.

You will begin to see that conjunctions (except for *and, or, but*) are, in a sense, similar to prepositions. They are indeed; and dependent clauses are quite similar to phrases. Consider the following sentence:—

The actor in the film played an outstanding role.
The actor who appeared in the film played an outstanding role.

In the first sentence, 'in the film' is an adjective phrase describing 'actor'. In the second sentence, 'who appeared in the film' is a clause performing the same role of adjective. Having a subject and finite verb, the clause can be shown in diagram as—

```
who———appeared
               \
                in the film
```

'Who' is considered to be the subject of the clause; 'appeared' is the simple past tense of the verb 'appear'; 'in the film' is an adverbial phrase. Such a clause should not be confused with a parciple phrase as in, 'The actor appearing in the film played an outstanding role.' Here 'appearing in the film' has no subject, no finite verb; it is a phrase, not a clause.

Dependent clauses play the role of an adjective, adverb or noun. Of the conjunctions used to introduce dependent clauses, two groups are given distinction—**relative pronouns** and **relative adverbs.**

RELATIVE PRONOUNS

The words *that, which* and *who* (or *whom*) not only join clauses together, but the words also stand-in for a noun or another pronoun. Consider their roles in the following sentences.

The girl *whom* you saw is my sister.
The idea *that* he presented was novel.
The car, *which* was rusted, fetched little.

In the first sentence, 'whom' not only stands-in for 'girl', it also introduces the dependent clause 'whom you saw'—'you' being the subject, 'saw' the verb, and 'whom' the object—'you saw whom'. (for use of *who & whom*, see index)

In the second sentence, 'that' stands-in for 'idea' while also introducing the relative clause 'that he presented' (subject, 'he'; verb, 'presented'). In the third sentence 'which' is a pronoun for 'car', and introduces the relative clause 'which was rusted'. Here, the word 'which' is itself subject of the verb 'was rusted'.

Each of these dependent clauses is related to a noun in the main clause by a pronoun—hence their name, relative pronoun. It might have occurred to you that the relative pronouns could have been omitted from the first two sentences with no loss of meaning, i.e. 'The girl you saw is my sister,' and 'The idea he presented was novel.' This is often the case. It becomes a trick in analysing sentences to see where the relative pronouns have been omitted (ellipsis), and re-insert them so as to understand better the job of various word-groups in the sentence.

RELATIVE ADVERBS

As you know, adverbs answer the questions Where, When, Why and How, and so, if a clause begins with these words, we might expect the clause to be adverbial in nature. But this is not always so. Consider the two following sentences:—

I will live where it is warm.

The place where I live is warm.

In the first sentence, 'where' introduces the relative clause 'where it is warm'. The clause *does* answer the question Where for the verb 'will live'; therefore it is a dependent clause acting as an adverb. In the second sentence, 'where' introduces the relative clause 'where I live', but here, it describes 'place'—which place?—where I live. It is, therefore, an adjective clause.

Dependent clauses play the role of an adjective, adverb or noun. By replacing a clause with a phrase (or better, a one-word equivalent), it is simple to find the function of a clause in a sentence. And to find the number of clauses in a sentence, we merely count the number of finite verbs. Let us put some of this information to work, first with the analysis of a sentence from the *Guinness Book of Records:—*

There is evidence that life expectation in Britain in the 5th century A.D. was 33 years for males and 27 years for females.

There are two finite verbs—'is' and 'was'—so there must be two clauses. Now let us simplify the sentence by omitting words and phrases that do not alter the grammatical structure of the sentence.

There is evidence that early life expectation was 33 and 27.

Obviously, 'There is evidence' (or more properly, 'Evidence is there') is an independent clause; the rest of the sentence is a dependent clause, and as such, is the equivalent of an adverb, adjective or noun. We might be led to believe that the clause 'that early life expectation was 33 and 27' was the equivalent of an adjective describing 'evidence'; but it isn't, it's a noun clause and, what is more, there is a simple way to tell. The dependent clause is a noun clause in apposition to 'evidence'. The whole sentence might be reduced to 'There is evidence, proof-positive.'

How can one immediately tell the difference between a noun clause and an adjective clause? If the relative pronoun can be replaced by another relative pronoun and still convey the same meaning, it is an adjective clause; but if such a substitution is *not* possible, it is a noun clause. Consider:—

The people whom I asked are friends = The people that I asked are friends.

The house that Jack built is solid = The house which Jack built is solid.

The clauses in each sentence are adjectival because another relative pronoun can be substituted, but in the two following sentences, no such substitution is possible—they are therefore noun clauses. 'I wish that he were here,' 'News that the king had died was broadcast in every country.' In the first sentence, 'that he were here' is a noun clause, object of the verb 'wish'; in the second sentence, 'that the king had died' is a noun clause in apposition to the subject, 'news'. In both of these sentences the word 'that' is not considered to be a relative pronoun, but merely a subordinating conjunction (a conjunction of the type that introduces a dependent clause).

Back now to our original sentence. Regarding the dependent clause as being a noun clause in apposition to the subject 'evidence' we might show the complete sentence in the diagram form thus:

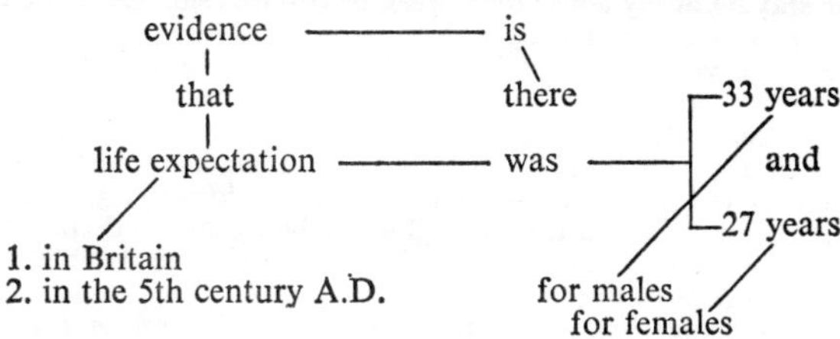

Let us try another sentence from R. L. Stevenson's ***Dr. Jekyll and Mr. Hyde***:—

They mounted the stair in silence, and still, with an occasional awestruck glance at the dead body, proceeded more thoroughly to examine the contents of the cabinet.

The finite verbs are 'mounted' and 'proceeded'; therefore we have two clauses. 'They mounted the stair in silence,' is an independent clause. 'Proceeded more thoroughly to examine the contents of the cabinet,' is another independent clause, which, through *ellipsis*—the omitting of words that are 'understood'—has lost its subject, 'they'. The intended meaning of the sentence then is, 'They mounted the stair in silence, and still, with an occasional awestruck glance at the dead body, *they* proceeded . . . '

'Proceeded' is an intransitive verb needing no object; therefore 'to examine the contents' is an infinitive adverb phrase describing 'proceeded'. 'Still' is another adverb—'still proceeded'. Again, 'with an occasional awestruck glance' tells *how* they proceeded—so does 'more thoroughly'; both are adverbs. 'At the dead body' describes 'glance', and is therefore an adjective phrase. Check each point of the following diagram.

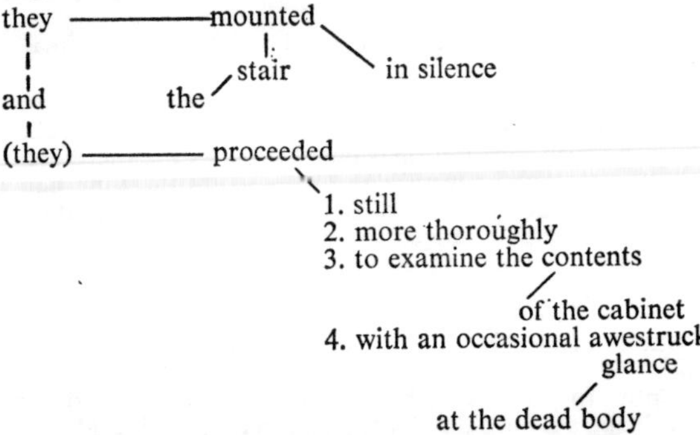

Try one more: **The delightful people I met in Malaga, Spain, will be staying at my house for a week or two this summer while their daughter is being married.**

The finite verbs are 'met', 'will be staying', 'is being married' (the last two express continuing action), so there are three clauses. Let us reduce the sentence to manageable proportions: 'People I met in Spain will be staying here while their daughter is being married.' The three clauses are 1. people will be staying here, 2. I met in Spain, 3. while their daughter is being married. But there is something wrong. The second clause is obviously dependent; it describes 'people', but it has no conjunction. The answer, once again, is ellipsis; 'whom' is to be understood—'*whom* I met in Spain'.

As mentioned, 'whom I met in Spain' is an adjective clause; a one-word equivalent would be 'Spanish'. What kind of people? *Spanish* people, (though, of course, they *might* have been English people).

'While their daughter is being married' could be reduced to the phrase 'during their daughter's wedding' and as such is seen to tell *when* they will be staying—an adverb. Here is a diagram of the entire sentence:—

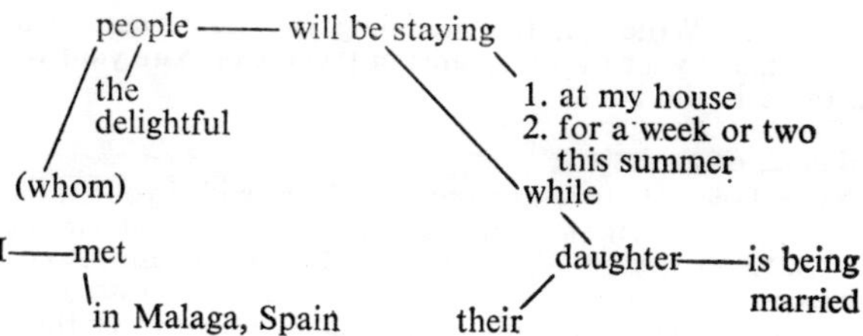

Let us end clause analysis with a long sentence from *Oliver Twist:—*

> **They had some cold meat for dinner; and sat there so long after it, while Mr. Sikes indulged himself with three of four pipes, that Oliver began to feel quite certain they were not going any further.**

With a sentence of this length it would be wiser to diagrammatise the parts separately rather than attempt to present them in a combined form. Verify the following analysis.

they — had — for dinner
had — meat
meat: 1. some 2. cold

and—joins the two main clauses

(they) — sat
sat: 1. there 2. long after it

while—introduces adverb clause describing 'sat'

Mr. Sikes — indulged
indulged: himself; with three or four pipes

so . . . that—'so' is an adverb describing 'sat' and helps introduce the conjunction 'that', which, in turn, introduces a clause of result limiting the verb 'sat'.

Oliver — began
began: to feel
to feel: certain
certain: quite

The following clause with or without 'that' understood, is a noun clause object to the infinitive 'to feel'.

they — were going
were going: 1. not 2. any further

Final test: Write out the preceding four sentences, then tomorrow, make your own diagrams of them. Compare your results with those in the book.

Final notes on analysis

The analysis of long sentences is simple, provided you: 1. reduce the sentence to a simple form, 2. put the words in their proper order, 3. 'shop around' for equivalent words or phrases. A correct analysis is one based on logic; but that doesn't necessarily mean two experts will come up with identical analyses. Any well-thought-out analysis based on what you have learned up to this point will be correct, or should be very close to it.

Part Six

PUNCTUATION

PUNCTUATION IS OFTEN a matter of personal taste. Instead of a lengthy list of rules, here are a few general words of guidance.

The **full-stop** or **period** is placed at the end of every sentence (provided a question mark or exclamation mark is not required). Full-stops follows abbreviations—etc., 10 oz., B.A.—though they are often omitted from Mr, Mrs, and Dr. Numbers 1, 2, 3 and etc. are not regarded as abbreviations, nor are the ordinal numbers—1st, 2nd, 3rd—so no full-stop is required.

The **comma** is a brief pause which gives detachment to individual words or groups of words: He sells the fish, and I sell the chips; We have some nice, fresh, tasty, filleted cod; My father, who started this shop, went out and caught the fish himself. The preceding sentences show detachment of words, detachment of groups of words, and the detachment of a commenting clause (*see page* **44**). An absolute phrase (*page* **43**) must *not* include a comma.

The **semi-colon** (;) provides a longer pause than the comma; it permits the joining of short related thoughts; often makes a conjunction unnecessary, and avoids a string of brief sentences—as it has done in this sentence.

The **colon** (:) is used mainly to introduce a list of items: bread, butter, chicken. A **dash** is used for an abrupt change in the construction of a sentence: e.g. 'Martha was having her hair done when—but I think I'd better let her tell you herself.' A pair of dashes—as here—is used for parenthesis. A single dash at the end of sentence is may be used for an example, a comment or a summing up of the sentence—again, as here.

When words are enclosed in **quotation marks**—either 'single' or "double"—punctuation is placed *within* the quotation marks if it serves the needs of both the quoted material and the main sentence: The sentence 'John is here,' contains a linking verb. Notice the linking verb in 'John is here.'

As readers, we tend to take punctuation very much for granted. The best way to gain familiarity with the various marks and their uses, is to study a printed page—*this* page, if you like—and question each mark used.

The rest of this section deals with some of the:—

WORDS AND EXPRESSIONS FREQUENTLY CONFUSED

Who—Whom

These two words cause far too much trouble. Misuse of one for the other as in 'Who is it for?' is accepted usage; however, here are the *correct* usages.

'Who' is in the subjective role or case, 'whom' is objective. This means 'who' is suitable for use as a subject, 'Who killed Cock Robin?' or as the balance (complement) of a linking verb, 'Who do you think you are?' (You do think you are who). 'Who is it?' (It is who).

On the other hand, 'whom' is correct for object to the verb, 'You told whom?' or as the object of a preposition—*to whom, for whom, from whom, with whom, by whom.* Confusion arises easily however, when 'whom' is separated from the preposition governing it, and so we hear, 'Who is this for?' 'Who is it addressed to?'

The errors above can be avoided with a little forethought, but the choice becomes more puzzling when it arises mid-sentence. The italicised word in each of the following quotations should be 'who'.

> '. . . to displace their leader by someone *whom* they imagined would be a more vigorous President.' (SIR WINSTON CHURCHILL)
>
> '. . . a creature *whom* we pretend is already here.' (E. M. FORSTER)
>
> 'Bateman could not imagine *whom* it was that he passed off as his nephew.' (SOMERSET MAUGHAM)

When men of this stature confuse 'who' and 'whom', the rest of us might well wonder if we are capable of mastering the difference. In the first example, 'whom' is posing as the subject of the verb 'would be'. Confusion arises because of the insertion of 'they imagined'. Remove these two words and it becomes immediately obvious that 'who' is required rather than 'whom'.

Similarly, in the second sentence, remove the words 'we pretend' and it is seen that 'who' is required as subject for the verb 'is'. In the third example, the clause is 'it was who'—the linking verb 'was' requires the *subjective* form be used rather than the objective form 'whom'.

That—Which—Who—relative pronouns (*see page* **47**)

These three words are pronouns; they stand-in for nouns. 'Who' can represent only people; 'which' can represent only things; 'that' can represent either people *or* things.

'Who' (or **'whom'**) is used to introduce commenting clauses as in: 'My wife, who bought the dress, has good taste.' 'Who' and 'whom' can also introduce describing clauses: e.g. 'The man who is there is her father.' 'The man whom you saw is her father.'

'That' can replace 'who' or 'whom' in a describing clause: e.g. 'The man that is there is her father.' 'The man that you saw is her father;' but it cannot replace 'who' or 'whom' in a commenting clause, i.e. 'My wife, that bought the dress, has good taste.'

'Which' is best suited for commenting clauses: e.g. 'His innocence, which has still to be proven, would establish a precedence in murder cases;' though it is rarely *un*suitable for use in describing clauses—as it is here: 'All which I have is yours.' Briefly: use 'who' to introduce commenting clauses for people; use 'which' mainly to introduce commenting clauses for things; use 'that' to introduce describing clauses for both people and things.

Plurals and possession

The words *sheep, deer, reindeer, grouse, moose, salmon, trout* are both the singular and plural forms. 'Fish' may be singular or plural; 'fishes' usually refers to varieties.

Compound nouns usually add S to their most important word; thus, *brother-in-law* becomes *brothers-in-law; court-martial* becomes *courts-martial; commander-in-chief* becomes *commanders-in-chief.*

Nouns form their possessive case by adding 'S. The bicycle belonging to a boy is therefore 'a *boy's* bicycle'. When the noun already ends with S, it adds an apostrophe; another S is optional; thus *James'* or *James's, princess'* or *princess's, boss'* or *boss's.*

If a noun is plural but it does not end with an S, then again add 'S to show ownership: e.g. *men's, women's, children's, people's.* But if the plural form ends with S, add only the apostrophe—*neighbours', friends', relatives', lions'.*

Some expressions of time and some idiomatic expressions may be possessive: e.g. *a day's work, a week's pay, a month's holiday, for goodness' sake.*

The possessive form should be used before gerunds.

WRONG: There's small chance of *John* seeing him. (use *John's*)
RIGHT: *Your* having a car is very handy.
WRONG: Do you mind *me* telling him this. (use *my*)

Whose and who's

'Who's' is a contraction of 'who is'; 'whose' is a possessive pronoun.

RIGHT: Whose car is this?
RIGHT: Who's the girl?

Its and it's

'It's' is a contraction of 'it is'; 'its' is a possessive pronoun.

RIGHT: It's for you.
RIGHT: What is its name?

Except and excepting

'Excepting' is for negative use—for a situation in fact which names something that is *not* to be excepted.

RIGHT: Every country in the world—not excepting even the smallest—has right of voice concerning radioactive fallout.

RIGHT: All the girls except Mary finished the project in time.
WRONG: All the apples are wormy excepting this one. (use *except*)
WRONG: Excepting the views expressed by the chairman, the meeting was just an informal chit-chat. (use *except for*)

Than

'Than' is a conjunction, though ellipsis (omission) sometimes makes it seem a preposition. If you add the verb in your mind, you won't confuse the case.

WRONG: She is taller than me. (than *I am*)
RIGHT: He is more intelligent than she (is).

Will—Shall

'Shall' expresses simple futurity for 1st person singular and plural ('I' and 'we'): e.g. 'I shall go to London tomorrow if it is nice,' 'We shall be married in August.' 'Will' expresses simple futurity for all other persons: e.g. 'You/he/they will be very welcome.' However, the roles of the words reverse for determination or command: e.g. 'I *will* go in spite of what you say,' 'He *shall not* have his way in this matter.'

As if—as though

These expressions need be followed by a verb that expresses uncertainty, *not* fact.

WRONG: He speaks as if he can help. (the verb 'can' does not express uncertainty—use 'could')
RIGHT: She swam as if her life depended upon winning. (the speaker has no guarantee that her life did *not* depend upon winning. Only her psychiatrist knows for certain)
WRONG: It seems as though the squirrels know spring is near and find it all the more difficult to wait. (substitute *knew, was* and *found*)

Sit—Set

Present	Past	Past Participle
sit	sat	sat
set	set	set

The verb 'sit' expresses what humans do; the verb 'set' expresses what humans do *to* objects. See also 'lay—lie.'

WRONG: I'll just set a moment and rest my feet.
WRONG: Don't sit that flower-pot on the window-sill.

Like

This word may be used as a preposition but not as a conjunction.

RIGHT: You make me feel like a fool.
WRONG: You make me feel like I was a fool.

Bad—Badly

'Bad' is an adjective, 'badly' an adverb. The adjective should be used after a linking verb; thus, 'He is bad,' 'Don't feel bad.'

Lie—Lay

These are two different verbs having different meanings and different forms.

Present	Past	Past Participle	Present Participle
lie	lay	lain	lying
lay	laid	laid	laying

The verb 'lie' means to 'rest' or 'recline'. It is an intransitive verb. The verb 'lay' means to 'place' or 'set'; it requires an object. Confusion would be less if the past time of 'lie' were different in form from the present time of 'lay.'

WRONG: Lie it on the table. (use *lay*)

WRONG: I had just laid down when the telephone rang. (use *lain*)

RIGHT: I lay down this afternoon for a nap.

RIGHT: He laid the wood by the stove.

Note: there is no such word as 'layed'.

RIGHT: Lying in bed is all he thinks about.

RIGHT: Having laid the last tile, he began to collect his tools.

Transpire means 'to become known', but it is often mistaken for 'happen': the first sentence is correct then, the second, impossible.

RIGHT: The Minister's response quickly transpired by radio and television.

WRONG: The secret attack did not transpire as planned.

Aggravate means 'to make worse' *not* 'to annoy'.

WRONG: I have an aggravating cough. (annoying)

WRONG: She has an aggravating way of speaking. (annoying or unpleasant)

RIGHT: Sometimes a bandage merely aggravates a wound.

RIGHT: Defeat was aggravated by cries of 'Coward!'

As you see, one need already *have* an annoying condition before it can be aggravated.

Individual should not be used as a mere substitute for *man, woman* or *person.*

WRONG: What a strange individual!

WRONG: He's a cheery enough individual when he's had a few drinks.

Its correct use is to indicate *one* person, or a few people among many.

RIGHT: An individual has small voice against a mob.

RIGHT: Many members applauded, though individuals booed.

i.e. and e.g.

The abbreviation *i.e.* stands for *id est,* Latin, meaning 'that is'.

Use it only where the words to follow it will refine, define or narrow what it is you are referring to.

RIGHT: The most expensive cups, i.e. the bone china, were broken first.

E.g. (*exempli gratia*) means 'for the sake of example' and introduces illustrations or instances which bear out the truth of a statement.

RIGHT: Often, the more delicate the item, the greater its cost; e.g. bone china.

The subtle difference between the two is that *i.e.* introduces something you had in mind from the beginning, whereas *e.g.* introduces something which was not specifically in mind, but which bears out the truth of the statement.

Historic and historical

A *historical* event is simply something that has happened. A *historic* event is something of great importance that has happened. When Bleriot flew across the English Channel in 1909, it was both a historical and historic event. But when the *next* man flew the Channel, it was only a historical event.

Answers to the Questions

PAGE 8

The sentences are numbers 1, 4, 5, 9, 10

PAGE 9

The nouns are numbers 1, 2, 6, 7, 10

PAGE 12

1. v.i. 2. linking. 3. v.i. 4. linking. 5. v.t. 6. v.t.

PAGE 23

Q.1

```
            organ ——————————————— has
           /                       |
  1. the  /                       pipes
  2. in Liverpool Cathedral       /
                          10,936 /
```

Q.2

```
        sun————————————————————sets
       /                          \
  the /                            \ 1. never
                                     2. on my Gin
```

Q.3

```
        celebration——    marked
       /                   |     \
  1. the                solstice  \ in pre-Christian times
  2. traditional        /
  3. December     1. the
                  2. winter
```

Q.4

```
        battle——was——on Drummossie Moor, Inverness-
       /           \                         shire
  1. the            \ in 1746
  2. last
  3. pitched
  4. in England
```

Q.5

```
  dogs——————————are allowed
                           \
                            \ 1. not
                              2. in the shop
```

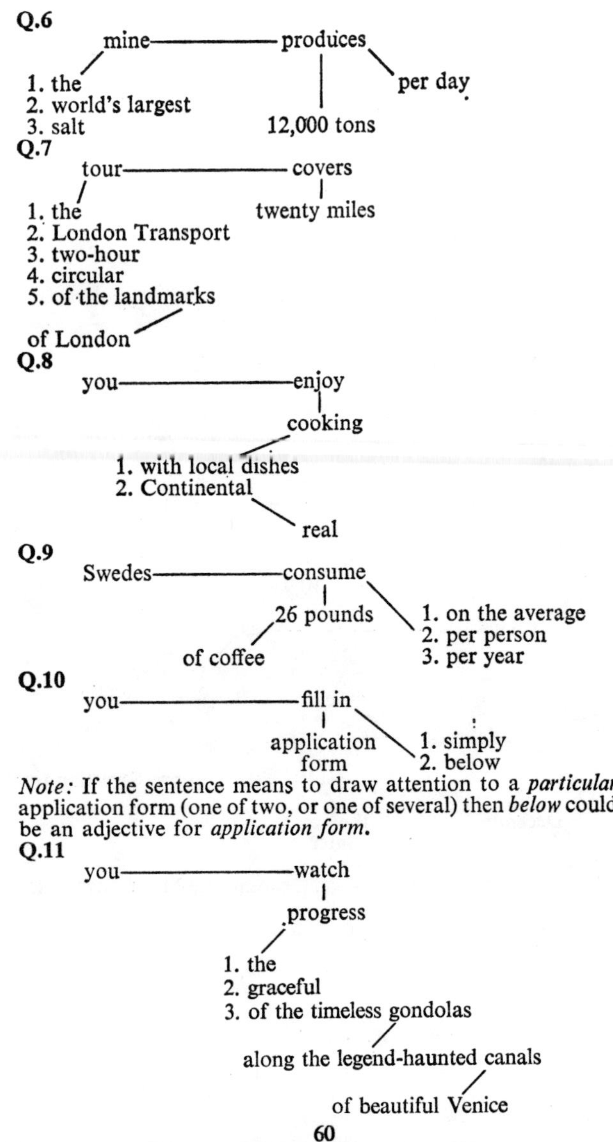

Note: If the sentence means to draw attention to a *particular* application form (one of two, or one of several) then *below* could be an adjective for *application form*.

PAGE 27

1. (you) are having—2nd p. sing. pres. cont. 2. (stitch) saves—3rd p. sing. pres. simple. 3. (they) are trying—3rd p. plural, pres. cont. 4. (you) have taken—2nd p. sing. pres. comp. 5. (buildings) will rise—3rd p. plural, future, simp. 6. (she) had been having—3rd p. sing. past, comp. cont. 7. (gut) provides—3rd p. sing. pres. simple. 8. (we) had been—1st p. plural, past comp. 9. (girls) have gone—3rd p. plural, past comp. 10. (they) have been trying—3rd p. plural, pres. comp. cont. 11. (he) will have been speaking—3rd p. sing. future, comp. cont.

PAGE 29

1. (raw sienna)—3rd p. sing. pres. simple, passive. 2. (they) 3rd p. plural, future, cont. active. 3. (Uranus) 3rd p. sing. pres. simple, passive. 4. (we) 1st p. plural, past completed, passive. 5. (travel) 3rd p. sing. past, simple, passive. 6. (newspaper) 3rd p. sing. present, simple. active. 7. (dam) 3rd p. sing. past, simple, passive. 8. (ship) 3rd p. sing. future, simple, passive. 9. (car) 3rd p. sing. pres. cont. passive.

PAGE 31

The following changes need be made: 1. were, 3. were, 6. were, 9. were.

PAGE 36

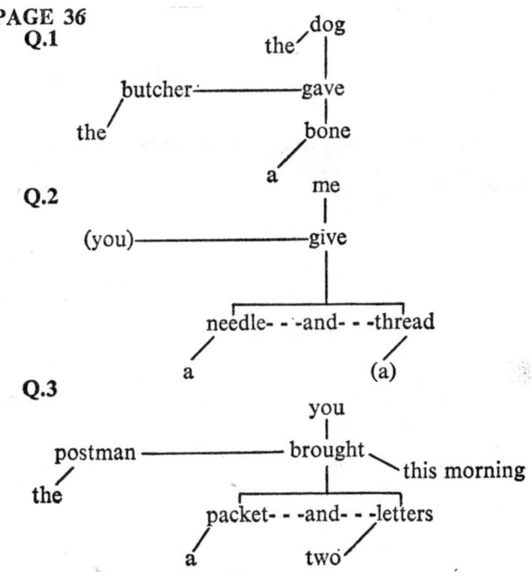

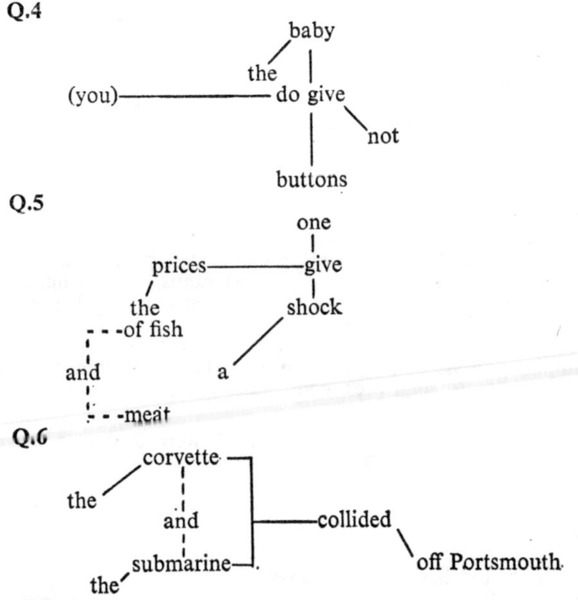

PAGE 45

1. *to . . . king*—infin. noun object. 2. *wearing . . . tunics*—pr. participle—*girls*. 3. *The . . . left*—absolute; *for another*—prep. noun object. 4. *through . . . window*—prep. adv.—*shouted*. 5. *Having . . . letters*—comp. participle—*she*. 6. *in . . . soil*—prep. adv.—*will grow*. 7. *Having . . . MPH*—comp. participle (passive)—*swift; in the world*—prep. adj.—*bird*. 8. *of . . . scale*—prep. adj.—*use; for . . . speeds*— prep. adj.—*scale; by . . . Acherer*—prep. noun-object; *of Zurich*—prep. adj.—*Professor Acherer*. 9. *All . . . considered*—absolute. 10. *To . . . area*—infin. noun-subject; *of a circle*—prep. adj.—*area*. 11. *to . . . chestnuts*—infin. noun-object. 12. *Reading a book*—gerund, subject. 13. *Feeling sorry*—gerund, subject; *for yourself*—prep. adv.—*sorry*. 14. *by wading*—prep. adv.—*have ruined; in puddles*—prep. adj.—*wading*. 15. *Tired . . . money*—dangling part; *buying a car*—gerund, subject. 16. *shared . . . eight*—past part.—*beer*. 17. *you . . . man*—infin. noun, object; *at all costs* (urgently)—prep. adv.—*want*. 18. *Help . . . arrived*—absolute. 19. *Having . . . means*—comp. part.—*he; battering the door*—gerund, object; *with a log* (destructively)—prep. adv.—*battering*. 20. *Dashed . . . rocks*—past part.—*Meredith; by rollers*—prep. adv.—*dashed; onto the beach*—prep. adv.—*staggered*.

Index

Index of words and expressions commonly confused